An Outbreak of Common Sense

Best wishes

An Outbreak of Common Sense
Robert Funning
Illustrated by Bekah

2017

Copyright © 2017 by Robert Funning

All rights reserved. This book or any portion thereof may not be reproduced or used in any manner whatsoever without the express written permission of the publisher except for the use of brief quotations in a book review or scholarly journal.

First Printing: 2017

ISBN 978-1-326-96974-5

Melbec Development Ltd
42, Briarigg
Kendal
LA9 6FA

www.melbecdevelopment.co.uk

Ordering Information:

Special discounts are available on quantity purchases by corporations, associations, educators, and others. For details, contact the publisher at the above listed address.

Dedication

To my loving wife, Sue, my beautiful girls and to all my friends who continually sharpen my thinking.

Contents

Introduction 3

Chapter 1
Taking a Strategic View 13

Chapter 2
Business Essentials 29

Chapter 3
Trust 49

Chapter 4
Create Partners 63

Chapter 5
Contracting 91

Chapter 6
Leadership and Management 105

Chapter 7
Leading people through change 125

Chapter 8
Management Basics 147

Chapter 9
Three Reasons Why We Don't Delegate 177

Chapter 10
Personal Effectiveness 197

Chapter 11
Effective Influence 225

Introduction

The world of organisational life can often seem bonkers. The latest, well intentioned, directive from on high can land like a lead balloon and leave you shaking your head in dismay.

I can remember one time I was part of a team running an intensive management course based on Dartmoor. The programme had been both physically and mentally demanding, pushing all of us to our limits. We had been reviewing the programme to date and whilst everyone had agreed it had been a tough couple of days, we could see real progress was being made. But then our senior manager started to behave in way that, to me, seemed bizarre. From seemingly nowhere he just lost the plot. He had a go at everyone's performance, nothing had been good enough and somehow this was symptomatic of everything that was wrong not only in the organisation but also in the world! He then listed several unreasonable demands that would have included us running feedback sessions with delegates at 2:00am! I couldn't make sense of it. He seemed to be talking about a completely different programme to the one that I had been on and his demands seemed to be completely bonkers.

When he left the room, I was left almost in a state of shock. His outburst had been deeply unsettling. One of the team had a psychology background and I turned to him to him to try and make sense of things.

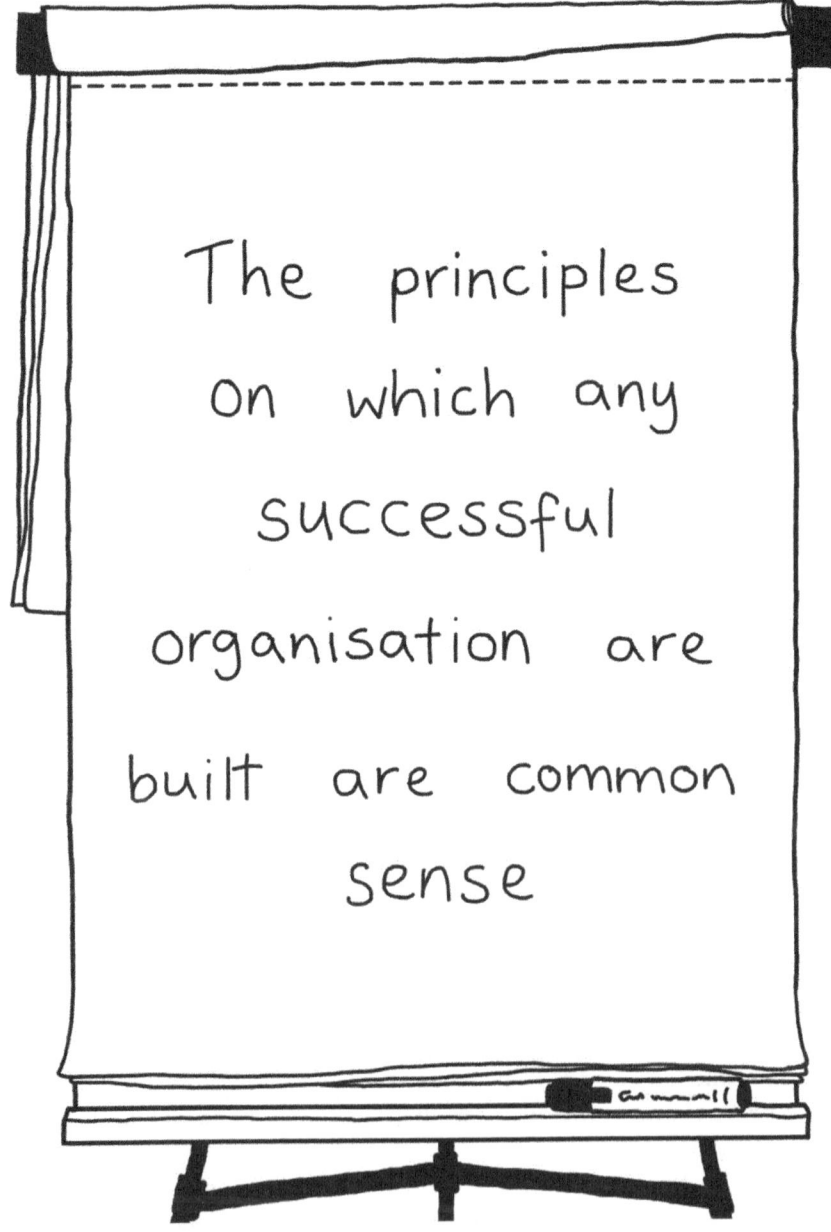

Introduction

'What just happened there?' I asked.

'When someone is behaving in a way that might be described as mad, you start to doubt your own reality,' he replied. 'You start asking yourself the question, is it just me or is this nuts? You find yourself reaching out to touch things that you know to be true to reassure yourself. For example, you might find yourself grabbing the edge of the table in front of you to check it's real.'

I have had many moments when I have found myself grabbing the edge of the table. On another occasion, during my time in retail banking, the Area Office decided it would be good idea to reward people for selling accident insurance by sending them a Mars Bar for each policy they sold. No, I didn't understand why either! It gets worse though. To keep costs down they decided to send each 'prize' through the internal post system. Imagine how encouraged I felt to receive my weekly supply of squashed chocolate through the post! Repeated experiences such as these left me longing for the headline in the latest internal news bulletin to be, 'An outbreak of common sense hit the Bank today!'

In the busyness of organisational life there is a great danger that we get lost in the noise of visions, strategies, initiatives, mission statements, operating plans and the like and forget the common-sense principles on which successful organisations of all types are built. For example, how about some of these for starters: -

- We must fit the world in which we live
- Successful businesses must do two things; have more money coming in than going out and be able to pay the bills on time.
- All organisations are built on relationships. Relationships are built on trust. The greater the trust, the better the organisation.
- The more engaged people are and the more they are encouraged to use their initiative, the more effective an organisation will be.
- We need to pay attention to both the task <u>and</u> our relationship if we are to be effective.
- Leaders make change happen and managers create order and stability.
- Change is both a logical and an emotional process; people don't always do just what logic dictates.

- Managers need to balance the needs of the task with the needs of the people. If you treat people like numbers, they will behave like numbers.
- Trust means taking a risk. Trust is only evident in our actions
- To be personally effective we must have balance in our lives.
- Effective influence is a two-way street. You won't be effective in your influence if you are not open to influence yourself.

Seems obvious doesn't it. Common sense, but often not common practice.

But what's on your mind? I am going to guess that some of the problems you are facing include some, or all, of the following: -

You are under pressure to keep on improving your results. You manage to scrape through one year and then your bosses want you to do 10% more next year! It's never ending. And to top it all they want you to do this whilst making cost savings to.

You have to make big changes. The world around you is changing fast and if you don't change, your organisation or department will soon become irrelevant. Trying to get people to recognise this is only half of the challenge. Even when they do get it, they still don't change. It drives you mad.

Your people just don't behave logically. It feels like you are herding cats. They play games with each other; you feel like you need a degree in organisational politics to survive. Why can't people just get on with each other and just do the job in hand?

It's taken years of hard work to build the reputation of your organisation but all this could be lost with one stupid mistake that would be all over social media in a second. And all of this is before lunch!! It's fun being a leader isn't it!!

During my career in developing leaders and helping organisations through major change, I have worked with a whole variety of different types of organisation around the world; multinationals, start-up businesses and SMEs, public sector bodies, hospitals, military organisations, schools and universities, churches, charities and 'not for profit' businesses. I am often asked how different these organisations are from one another. The answer is that they are more alike than you might at first think. The common factor in any organisation is people. When people get together to try and achieve

An Outbreak of Common Sense

Introduction

some common purpose or vision there is always going to be some fun and games.

This book is intended to be a straightforward resource of ideas, thoughts, models and hints and tips for anyone who has the responsibility to lead or manage people through all the fun and games of organisational life. It is intended that these ideas can be implemented by anybody, in any type of organisation and at any level. The book does not need to be read from cover to cover but you can just dip into chapters that seem relevant to your situation.

A Model for Leadership Effectiveness
I have structured the book around a simple model for leadership effectiveness (see over). The foundation for individual success in any organisation is that you 'know your stuff'; that you are technically competent (Operational Excellence). At one time this would almost have been all that you needed to be. As long as you did your job well, other people in the organisation could do the other stuff. Whilst operational excellence is still core, the focus of this book is on the three other areas required to be an effective manager or leader in an organisation seeking to survive/thrive in a fast-changing world.

You must 'know your world'; being aware of how things are changing and able to engage people in how you must respond to survive (Strategic View). You must 'know your numbers'; having an awareness of how what you are doing is affecting the bottom line performance of your organisation (Commercially Astute). You must 'know people'; being able to develop excellent relationships both inside and outside of your organisation (Relationship Excellence).

Chapter 1 looks at the strategic view and explores the dynamic relationship your organisation must have with the changing world around it.

Chapter 2 is centred on commercial astuteness and explores the essential principles that underpin any successful business. This includes charities, 'not for profit' businesses and increasingly, many public sector organisations and schools that are expected to run on a more commercial footing.

Chapters 3-11 look at a variety of different aspects of relationship excellence. All relationships are built on trust, so chapter 3 on this subject is core to all the following chapters. The remaining relationship excellence chapters are grouped by subject matter; Chapters 4-5 look at establishing

9

great leader/'follower' relationships, Chapters 6-7 look at leadership and leading people through change, Chapters 8-9 look at effective management and delegation, Chapters 10-11 look at personal effectiveness and influence.

Definitions

At the outset, I would also like to give you a quick heads up about my use of the terms leader, manager, follower and team member. As you will see in the chapter on the difference between leadership and management, I work to some simple definitions of the two; leadership is about creating change and management is about creating order and stability. I am aware that the labels of leader and manager are switched around regularly within most organisations but hopefully you will find these definitions pragmatic and useful within the book.

It's also true that if you are to be a leader then someone else must be a follower. You can't be a leader without having someone follow your lead! I do understand though, the label 'follower' may sound weak to many people. In my view this is far from the case. For a modern day organisation to thrive it must have courageous and effective leaders, managers and followers. I will however sometimes use the title 'team member' as opposed to 'follower', as this is often more acceptable in organisational life.

I do hope that you find this a useful resource as you seek to build a great organisation on a good old fashioned dose of common sense! If all else fails, you can always colour in the pictures; I hear that's quite popular these days!!

Chapter 1
Taking a Strategic View

We must fit the world in which we live

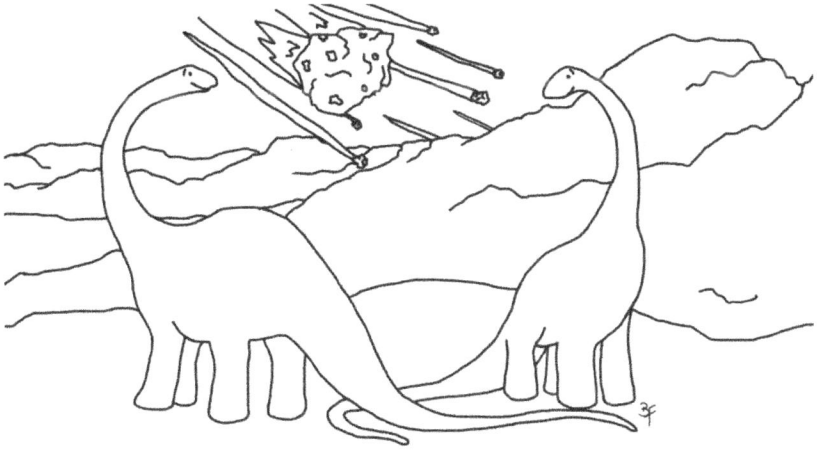

"So what are your plans for next week?"
"Oh you know, the same old, same old."

On the eve of their annual strategic senior team meeting an IT department in a multi-national company learnt that they need to make a 20% reduction in their budget over the next year. This would include two of their present number of ten also losing their jobs! The temptation to dump all things strategic and try to work this out was immense.

To his credit the leader held true to their original agenda. He realised that a short term fix might solve their immediate budgetary issues but what was required here was a more fundamental solution. The problem was not just surviving the next 12 months but building a department that met the needs of their fast changing organisation as it continued to evolve.

The team spent the first couple of hours acknowledging the emotional impact of the news, both on the team and the department, before committing to a process of fully understanding the changing world in which they were operating, and defining the critical principles that would not only

Of Squares and Triangles

Once upon a time the world was square. Right angles were definitely the order of the day. Into this world was born a little quadrilateral. It fitted the world perfectly; everybody loved it and welcomed it. As a result, it thrived and prospered. It grew bigger and bigger, all the time seeking to ensure that each one of its four sides were straight and equal and that each junction met at a perfect angle of 90°. It thrived; doing so well in fact that it gave birth to several smaller squares which also prospered. Life was good for the quadrilateral and it saw no reason as to why it should not continue to be so.

However subtly, slowly and almost imperceptibly the world was changing. The angle of choice was gradually reducing. 90° was no longer 'in' and a slow but relentless move was in progress to the new angle of choice, 60°. At first the quadrilateral didn't even notice the change, the drift to 60° was slow and what was the difference of 2 or 3 degrees between friends! The growth of the quadrilateral empire though started to slow. This was somewhat concerning to the quadrilateral that had been used to years of continued significant expansion. Meetings were convened, think tanks explored and figures analysed. Everyone came to the same conclusion........ this was just a blip, a mere hiccup on the path to world domination.

But in the world the shift towards the sharper angle of choice continued. Not even did the quadrilateral stop growing but horror of all horrors it even started to decline. The world was starting to be drawn to a new type of shape appearing on the block. A shape that seemed to have only three sides. More meetings were convened, more think tanks explored and more figures analysed. This time the conclusion...... there must have been a slip up in how well we have been doing our square! 'Make the sides straighter, check and double check the lengths, make sure everything is exactly 90°! Squares have always worked for us in the past and therefore we must work harder at making everything square!!'

But the feverish geometric activity failed to produce the desired results. Not only did the quadrilateral fail to reverse the decline; it accelerated! Panic set in. One could hardly move in the quadrilateral for feverish crisis meetings, think tanks and analysis. Eventually the truth dawned. The world was no longer square but triangular. The conclusion........ lose a side and lose it right now!

Well as is no surprise things did not turn out well for the quadrilateral. A square with only three sides is no shape at all and certainly no competition for the now well-formed equilateral triangles the world so much adored. The quadrilateral broke up and was no more.

Once upon a time the world was triangular and so the story continued.

see them through this crisis, but also shape a department 'fit for purpose' in the future. The department not only fulfilled its required budgetary cuts but over the next three years enhanced levels of staff engagement and was acknowledged both internally and externally to be delivering an exemplary level of service to the business.

Change or Die
From the very dawn of time one of the universal truths has been that success is linked to how well you fit the world in which you live. This has been as true for the rise and fall of dinosaurs in pre-historic times as to the growth and demise of modern day institutions, organisations and businesses.

This universal truth can be summarised in the quote, 'It is not the strongest of the species that survives, nor the most intelligent, but rather the one most adaptable to change.' It is estimated that 99.9% of all species that have ever existed on earth are now extinct! Change, survival and extinction are an ongoing part of life on earth. Perhaps some of the underpinning messages of this parable over the page may well ring true to you.

The message of this parable seems so obvious, common sense we might say. We must continually adapt to the changes in the world if we are to thrive or survive. Common sense but not, in my experience, common practice!

I have worked with a wide variety of private and public sector organisations even institutions such as the Church of England. One has only to look at the evidence of recent years to see the consequences for organisations that fail to adapt to changes in their world. In the private sector, over 70% of the companies that made up the original FTSE 100 list have now disappeared from the index having either failed, been acquired or slipped back into the second division of performance. This has happened over a space of around thirty years! Public sector organisations across the country are struggling to come to terms with the double whammy of increased demand for their services combined with declining tax revenues from an ageing population. The Church of England, which once had a central role in the life of society, has now become marginalised with dramatic declines in attendance being seen over the past 20-30 years. One has only to look at how many empty churches and chapels there are across the country to see how the church has failed to remain relevant to the world in which it lives.

Our love/hate relationship with change

So how can it be that if it is common sense that we must change in line with the world around us, is this so consistently overlooked by all forms of organisations? Well the common factor in any type of organisation is people and people have a love/hate relationship with change.

Imagine for a moment that you won the lottery and that you had the resources to create the lifestyle that you had always desired. Once you had lived that lifestyle for a bit, what do you think you would be likely to do? Well the chances are, even though you now had the lifestyle you always dreamt of, you would soon become bored with it and look to make some changes.

At one level, we love change. Change can be interesting, exciting, stimulating. If it is on our own terms we often enjoy learning new things and taking up different challenges. One of the core motivators for people is personal growth. We like it when we can look back and see that we have progressed from where we once were. However, we are also predisposed to avoid change. Two bits of caveman thinking that are deeply engrained in human psyche are, 'Stick to what you know' and 'Follow the crowds'.

In a world that was stable, or changed very slowly, this was brilliant logic. If you have found something that worked for you or worked for someone else, keep doing it. And if you wanted your offspring to survive, engrain in them the same thinking and behaviours. Fast forward a few millennia, we still think the same way but live in a world that changes almost unrecognisably within the space of one generation. Continuing to do the same thing in a changing world is certainly not a recipe for survival!

It has been evidenced across numerous psychological studies that we have an in-built bias towards maintaining the status quo over change. We outweigh the risks of trying something new and moving into unknown areas over the risks of staying as we are. This leads us often only to pursue change at the last minute, when the risks of staying where we are become overwhelming. How many times have you been part of an organisation where the first real response to evidence of decline is to carry on doing what has always been done but to do it harder!!? Or how many times have you seen, when this strategy fails, a sudden lurch to wholesale chaotic change with what feels like six million change initiatives and projects firing off at the same time like some out of control firework display?

The Six Monkeys in a Cage

So the tale goes, 6 monkeys were placed in a cage under experimental conditions. As part of the experiment a high platform was placed in the middle of the cage. Above the platform, they hung a bunch of beautifully ripe bananas. However, they also rigged sensors to the ladder that the monkeys had to climb to access the platform. These sensors, if triggered, set off powerful jets of water that would completely soak every monkey in the cage.

Now apparently, monkeys don't like getting wet. Each time one of them stepped on the ladder the torrent of water poured down. It didn't take them long to learn to avoid the ladder and to look for food elsewhere in the cage. After a while the experimenters turned the sensors off. The monkeys' world had changed but of course they didn't know it and so they continued to work to the belief that the ladder was best avoided.

As the experiment continued they decided to replace one of the original monkeys with one that had never been in the cage before. The new monkey on seeing the bananas hanging temptingly above the platform quickly went to climb the ladder. However, the five old remaining monkeys, thinking that they were about to get soaked, quickly communicated, in ways only a monkey can, that this was not a good idea and repeatedly mobbed the new monkey if it went close to the ladder. The new monkey soon gave up with the ladder idea and joined the other monkeys in their pursuit of food elsewhere.

Well the experiment continued and they went on replacing original monkeys with new ones and the same pattern of behaviour continued. They eventually got to the point where there were 6 new monkeys in the cage, none of which who had experienced the jets of water, but all who still avoided the ladder. If you could have asked them why they didn't go for the bananas above the platform they would have replied in best monkey speak,

'I don't know really, it's just the way that we do things around here!'

Group think

Another powerful factor that leads to organisations failing to adapt to change in their world in a timely fashion is something called group think. Where group think prevails the people within an organisation get stuck in the same views, beliefs and ways of working. People all see things the same way, so strongly in fact that they quickly dismiss or miss completely any alternative view.

This idea is beautifully illustrated in the tale of 'The 6 Monkeys in a Cage' detailed over. Whether this tale is true or not it illustrates a common truth within organisations. A group of people learn something from experience and soon this turns into a commonly held organisational belief. This belief may be very well founded, the original monkeys did have a bad experience, but the belief is never tested later to see if it is still valid. As new people join the organisation they are quickly indoctrinated to the unwritten rules of 'how we do things around here'. Challenge of the prevailing thinking is not welcomed and quickly people conform to fit in with the group.

Just for a moment think about the unwritten rules that you work to within your organisation. A useful way to do this is to complete the following sentences: -

In my organisation: -

- You should always ....
- You must ....
- You can ....
- You cannot ....
- We want ....
- We don't want ....
- We choose to ....
- We choose not to ....

As you reflect on the unwritten rules of your organisation think about how many of these rules, by which you operate, actually came from a direct experience you had! I reckon that someone new has about 6 months before they slip into the prevailing ways of thinking and behaviour within an organisation. It is a bit like meeting the Borg in Star Trek, 'You will be assimilated. Resistance is futile!'

Smart organisations seek to fully utilise the fresh perspectives that new people bring to broaden their view and to help them to adapt to potential unseen changes in the world. Do jets of water still spurt from the

An Outbreak of Common Sense

ceiling if we put a foot on the ladder? We often miss opportunities by failing to test if our world has changed.

So what

Well this is all fine and good, you might say, but what am I supposed to do with all of this? Well first we must maintain a balance between looking internally and looking externally. Much of our time in organisational life will focus on looking inside our organisation, looking at how we can keep everything on track and how we might improve it. However, we move into dangerous waters when 'looking internally' dominates our focus.

One thing that is certain is that the world is continually going to change. It is not question of 'if you will need to change' at some point but 'when you must change'. With this truth in mind you must also make certain that you are regularly looking externally to understand how the world is moving and then make the appropriate changes to respond to this.

A useful metaphor for this is running a ship. If we are all deep down in the engine room trying to make the ship go faster there is a fair chance that we might hit an iceberg! We also need people on the bridge looking out, assessing the changing sea conditions and navigating accordingly.

In considering our fit with the world around us we need to consider these type of questions: -

- What are the trends in our performance?
- Do we have to work harder to maintain the same levels of performance?
- Looking back, how has our world changed over the past year or so?
- What have we done to respond to these changes?
- Looking forward, how do we expect the world to change?
- How might we need to respond to put ourselves in the best place to respond to that?
- What sort of feedback are we getting from all the stakeholders/interested parties in our organisation e.g. our customers, staff, shareholders, suppliers etc.?
- How is this feedback changing over time?
- What are the unwritten rules that we operate by and the assumptions that we are making about the world we operate in?
- Are these still valid and how do we know this?

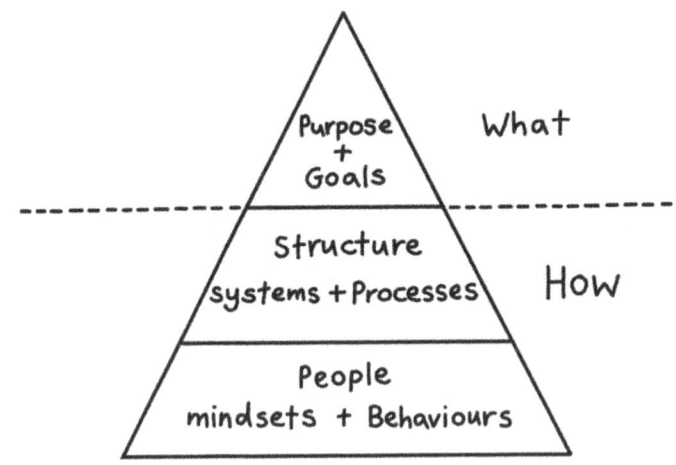

Simple model of an organisation

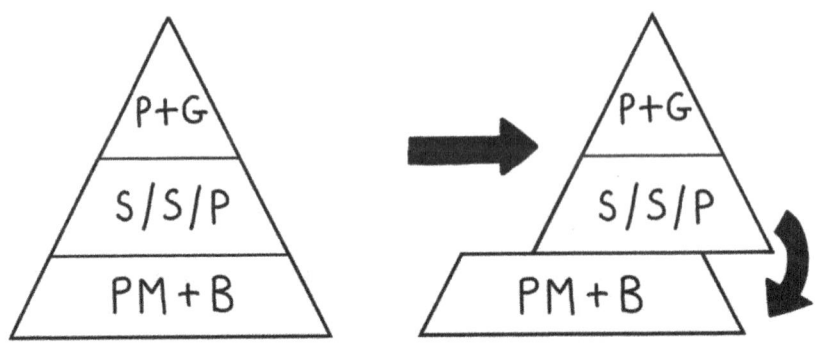

The danger of change without engaging people

Exploring questions such as these will give you a pretty good understanding of your world and the scale of change required for your organisation to ensure that you remain a good fit.

Building and organisation fit for purpose

The next critical step for changing your organisation is to define what 'shape' it needs to be to fit your changing world. A simple way to do this is to break your organisation down into three parts (see diagram over page): -

- **Purpose & Goals** – What is your organisation here to do and what are you seeking to achieve in the short, medium and long term?
- **Structure, Systems & Processes** – How will you organise yourself and go about your work?
- **People – mindsets, behaviours & skills** – How will you need your people to think and act if you are to be successful?

So, as you look at how your world is changing you need to ask three broad questions. How might your organisation's goals or areas of focus need to change? How might your organisation's structure, systems and processes need to change? And last, but by no means least, how might your people need to change?

When seeking to bring about organisational change it is very easy to focus too much on the upper parts of the organisational pyramid i.e. the goals and the structure, systems and processes. These often feel more tangible and easier to influence than trying to change people's thinking and behaviour. It is much easier to agree new goals, produce a new organisational chart or introduce a new system than it is to change the culture of your organisation. However, all these areas are interlinked. If people don't get the point of a change, they won't work to the new structure or implement the new systems in the way that you would want them to.

It has been estimated that over 70% of major organisational change initiatives fail to deliver the change they set out to achieve. The prime reason for this is failing to change the people. If you only work on the top two levels, you are in danger of creating a wobbly pyramid i.e. you shift the top layers without shifting the bottom one (see over page). This is not a recipe for organisational success! We will explore more about how we might engage people in change in later chapters.

An Outbreak of Common Sense

'Dad you are so square.
You have got to get with the times.'

When and how fast should we change?
The process of refining the 'shape' of your organisation must continually be revisited to keep track of changes in the world in which you live. If an organisation is to thrive it must be in 'dynamic balance' with the world around it i.e. it needs to be changing as quickly or as slowly as the world around it is changing. Clearly the most challenging time for any organisation is when change in the world is fast and/or substantial.

Organisations commonly underestimate the amount of time and effort required to bring about transformational change. Changing an organisation can be likened to trying to navigate a super tanker. One of these maritime beasts may take up to 5 miles to stop and even longer to get them pointing in a radically different direction! In my experience, even with concerted effort and good leadership, it might take up to 5 years to bring about transformational change within a sizeable organisation.

Balancing the operational world with the long term strategic view
It is critical that an organisation looks beyond just short term operations when seeking to understand how its world might be changing. This might mean that you need to consider change even when things seemingly are progressing ok. Despite the continued success of an organisation depending on having a longer term view, the short term operational agenda has dominated the focus of most senior teams that I have ever worked with.

None of the questions needed to take a strategic view are revolutionary. They are just common sense. The truth is this type of questions seems a bit ambiguous to most of us. The questions don't always lead to nice neat answers and invariably point to the fact that in some way that we must change. And change is such a pain in the backside. It means that we are going to have to invest significant amounts of time, effort and resources to reorder things. It means things are going to feel messy and untidy for a time. And this is all going to have to be done against the backdrop of still having to deal with the daily challenges of keeping the organisation afloat!

Building and sustaining highly effective organisations doesn't require high intellect but discipline. Discipline to avoid the traps such as sticking to what we know and group think. Discipline to battle the lure of staying with the known, short term challenges of daily operations. Discipline to step back, reflect, define and implement effective change strategies. The stark choice that all organisations ultimately face is change or die.

Ideas for action
Map your world
Either on your own or with your team, take a sheet of flipchart paper and jot down all the factors that may affect your world over the next 2-3 years. Consider the following: -
- How might economic changes affect your organisation?
- What political/legal changes may happen?
- How might technological changes affect your organisation?
- How might changes in society affect your organisation?
- What changes might affect how relevant your organisation is perceived in the world?
- As you look at your list of factors note what might be the opportunities and what might be the threats for your organisation.

Review the shape of your organisation?
Either on your own or with your team, take a sheet of flipchart paper and jot down how your organisation might need to change over the next few years to remain relevant in your world. Consider the following questions: -
- By what percentage might you need to change or refocus the goals of your organisation? Give some examples
- By what percentage might you need to change the structure and the systems/processes of your organisation? Give some examples
- By what percentage might you need to change the thinking and what people do in your organisation? Give some examples

As you look at these three questions, overall by what percentage might your organisation need to change over the coming years? What might the top three things be that will need to change first?

Personal challenges
Book 1-2 days out to review the strategic position of your organisation or division with a team of people drawn from across the organisation. Make this happen within the next 16 weeks.

Take 15 minutes out this week to reflect on the assumptions you have been working to e.g. I must/must not, I want/don't want, I choose/choose not, I can/cannot. Consider the impact these unwritten rules are having on you; what might need to change?

Summary of Taking a Strategic View
- Success is built upon fitting the world around us
- We have a love/hate relationship with change
- A common trap we can fall into is 'group think' when we all see the world the same way and fail to respond to change
- We need to balance looking internally, within our organisation, and externally, at the world around us
- We need to balance a short term operational view with a long term strategic view
- The time to consider transformational change may well be when things are still going well
- Three questions that help explore how you might need to change your organisation are: -
    o How might your organisation's goals or areas of focus need to change?
    o How might your organisation's structure, systems and processes need to change?
    o How might your people need to change?
- We need to change as fast as the world around us
- Change or die

Chapter 2
Business Essentials

To be a successful in business you need to do two things; have more money coming in than going out and be able to pay your bills on time

'The Tax man was unimpressed with Dave's creative offer to cover the VAT bill'

The core principles of business are not rocket science. In the UK, there are currently over 6,000,000 businesses. Most of the people running these businesses have never done an MBA, hold no accountancy qualifications and probably never have even read Business for Dummies! The core principles of running a business are intuitive and simple. To be successful in business you need to do two things. Wait for it. Here come these two gems of profound thinking and reasoning. To be successful in business you need to have more money coming in than going out and you need to be able to pay your bills on time.

'Oh, thank you great and wise guru' I hear you cry, 'we would have never worked that out by ourselves.' Whilst we can add a bit more detail to

Creating business partners

A hotel chain was wrestling with how they might implement an increase in wages, brought about by a change in government regulations, without adversely affecting the ongoing profitability of the business. The senior team decided that the best way that they could solve this problem would be to involve the staff in finding the solutions. Their thinking was how they solved the problem was as important as the solutions themselves. If they could get their staff to think more like business people, then this would not only be good for dealing with this wage increase, but also benefit the long term performance of the business.

Together we designed a one-day workshop that introduced 8 teams of 5 people, drawn from different parts of the chain, to the core business essentials principles. After the workshop the teams had 4 weeks, with coaching support from one of the senior managers, to come up with their ideas as to how they could cover the wage increase for their part of the business. Their brief was not only to come up with great ideas to increase the profitability of the business but also to show how they had engaged all the staff in coming up with these ideas. They were seeking to create business partners.

After the four weeks, each of the teams presented back both their ideas and their working. The senior management team had hoped to see ideas that might generate in the region of £100k to cover the wage increase. On the day, the 40 people presented back over 200 ideas to improve the profitability of the business with an estimated value of over £700k. Ideas ranged from longer term projects and investments to quick win ideas that had already been implemented in the four-week period. The buzz in the room was amazing. People had become involved in the 'game', they saw that what they did could make a real difference and had been actively encouraged to do this by the senior management team.

The staff's perspective had shifted from, 'we work for your business' to 'this is our business' and improvement in engagement and performance was immediate.

Business Essentials

these two principles, at its heart, whether you are a multinational business or Sammy the 'Shammy', the one man window cleaning operation, running a successful business is never more complicated than doing these two things.

Why then, if the fundamentals of business are so straight forward, do most large organisations fail to get their staff to think and act like business people? The prevailing thinking seems to run along the lines of; Sales and Marketing will get the work in, Operations will make sure it's delivered on time and Finance will make sure that all of that is done profitably and that the books balance.

Every decision and action, made by every person within a business, will influence the bottom line performance. Brian Clough, the colourful football manager of the late 20th Century, was once asked for his views on the controversial rule that a player wasn't offside if he wasn't interfering with play. His reply in typical Cloughy style was, 'If they are not interfering with play, I want to know what they were doing on the pitch in the first place!' The same is true in a modern-day business, if you are not affecting the performance of the business why are you there?! An illustration of what might be achieved by shifting this mindset is detailed in the story, Creating business partners, over the page.

So, let's look at how we might break the essentials of business down into manageable parts so that everyone can engage in it. The shorthand for the two core business principles is profit and cash. Both are equally important and critical to the success of your business. Clearly a business that is not profitable will not have a long and sustained future but neither will a business, which is profitable on paper, but hasn't got the cash available at the right time to pay its bills. Your staff, suppliers or the tax man will not take kindly to being asked to wait for payment whilst you try to flog some stock or get the money in that is owed to you by your customers. As many businesses fail for lack of cash as for lack of profit.

Despite this truth most business people focus more on profit than on cash. In fact, most business people don't even focus on profit but fall into the trap of chasing sales. If you ask someone to tell you about their business they will invariably tell you what their turnover is. 'We are a £20,000,000 business,' they might say seeking to impress. Well, it's not so impressive if you are making no profit for all that work. Running a business without making a profit is just being a busy fool. People chase sales for many reasons. Size is equated with success; inflated egos fuels the pursuit of sales;

Simple Profit + loss Statement

Sales £ X
Direct (variable) costs £ X

Gross Profit £ X
Overheads (fixed costs)

£ X

Net Profit £ X

people are fearful of having quiet times with staff and machines with no work therefore chase business at any cost. There is truth in the maxim that, 'Turnover is vanity and profit is sanity'. To this though should also be added, 'Cash is reality'.

Having more money coming in than going out (profit)

Expressed in its simplest terms profit is income less costs. When managing a business, it is helpful though to break down the various costs to see where the money is going. This is usually done by preparing a Profit and Loss Statement (see over).

The first line of the Profit and Loss statement is Sales. This is the income you derive from selling your goods or services. From this figure, we deduct the costs of running the business. These costs we split into two groups; 1) Costs that go up or down directly in line with the volume of sales. These are called Direct or Variable costs. 2) Costs that tend to remain relatively fixed no matter how much you sell. These are called Overheads or Fixed costs.

Examples of direct costs might include materials if you are making something or contract labour costs, people you hire to do a specific piece of work. By deducting the direct costs from your sales figure, you can work out your Gross Profit.

Gross profit = Sales - Direct Costs

Gross profit is sometimes called the real income of the business. Some people when monitoring their business like to calculate gross profit as a percentage of the sales figure (GP/Sales x 100). This percentage is called the Gross Profit Margin and tells you how much gross profit you are making for every pound of sales. You can track the gross profit margin as an indicator of how well the business is managing its pricing and controlling its direct costs. Whether your margin is going up or down is not necessarily a good or a bad thing. For example, you could improve your margin by putting up your prices, but putting up your prices may lose you work. Conversely, operating at a lower margin may be ok if this enables you to secure a higher volume of work.

The overheads or fixed costs of a business are those costs that are less directly linked to changes in sales. For example, things like salaries, rent & rates, utility bills must be paid if you sell nothing or if you sell a lot.

The Price is Right

When I was working as a bank manager one of my customers ran a small garage in the town. The business had been in his family for several years and had a regular band of loyal customers, all who valued the relationship of trust that they had with him. Financially though he was struggling. The business was at best breaking even and over time had built up sizeable debts.

I asked him what he was charging per hour for his work and how he had come to this figure. He said that he was charging about £25 per hour and that this was based, at the time, on what it might cost a customer to get their car serviced in one of the larger 'value' car servicing operators in the town. Here was his mistake; he assumed that he was in competition with every other business that provided car servicing in the town. This ranged from main dealers, the national chain servicing operators and other small garages like his. Whilst at first sight you could see why he thought these businesses were competition, when you looked a bit further though this was not the case.

People, with cars out of warranty, tend to get their cars serviced at one of the three different types of garage. Some people use the main dealer as they believe that they are the market leader for servicing their make of car. They are willing to pay increased prices for this perceived expertise. Other people use the large national chain operators primarily because they are looking to get the work done cheaply. The rest of the people use garages, like his own, because they value the relationship of trust that they have. Customers of each different type of garage rarely, if ever, think about taking their car to a different type of operation as it doesn't provide the value that they are looking for.

To reinforce the point that he wasn't in competition with the 'value' operators I asked him if any of his customers had ever asked him what his hourly rate was or queried what he had charged them for their service. He said that this rarely happened. Price wasn't the biggest issue for his customers.

I told him that I thought that he should consider increasing his prices. At first, he was extremely reticent to do this for fear of losing business. When we explored it though we saw that even if he went as far as doubling his prices this would only add around £50 to the average basic service, an increase that most of his customers wouldn't even notice or query.

He went away agreeing to apply a 50% increase to his prices. Within 12 months he had completely paid off his borrowing, had a healthy credit balance showing on his account and had even been able to take on some additional staff to have some long overdue family holidays; all of this without losing or upsetting any of his long standing customers.

Whilst we call these fixed costs they will vary somewhat in line with sales. What you tend to see are step changes in these types of costs as sales change e.g. if you grow your business, at some point you will probably have to take on extra staff or new premises. This will lead to a stepped increase in the overheads of your business. By deducting your overheads from your gross profit, you get your net profit.

$$\text{Net profit} = \text{Gross profit} - \text{Overheads}$$

Net profit is the bottom line and is the proof, or not, that you have had more money coming into the business than going out. As with gross profit some people like to express net profit as a percentage of sales when monitoring their business (NP/Sales x 100). This percentage is called the Net Profit Margin and can be tracked as an indicator of how well the business is managing its pricing and controlling its overheads.

The need to be profitable is also true for the growing number of social enterprises or sometimes called 'not only for profit' businesses. Whilst these types of businesses are not interested in making someone rich, they do still need to show a profit to be able to fund the continued development of the business. We will explore this further when we look at funding cash requirements within a business.

Four ways to increase your profit

Within the two business essentials principles of profit and cash, there are a few simple rules. These often seem to be rules of four. The first rule is that there are four ways that you can increase the profit of a business. These are common sense, they are: -

1. Sell more
2. Put your prices up
3. Reduce your costs
4. Change the mix of what you sell (i.e. sell more of the things you make more profit on)

Any strategy looking to increase the profitability of a business is never more complicated than following one, or a combination of, these four routes. The tricky thing is finding the right strategy for your world. The example over the page highlights the benefits of experimenting with your pricing strategy to maximise profits.

Cash Eaters

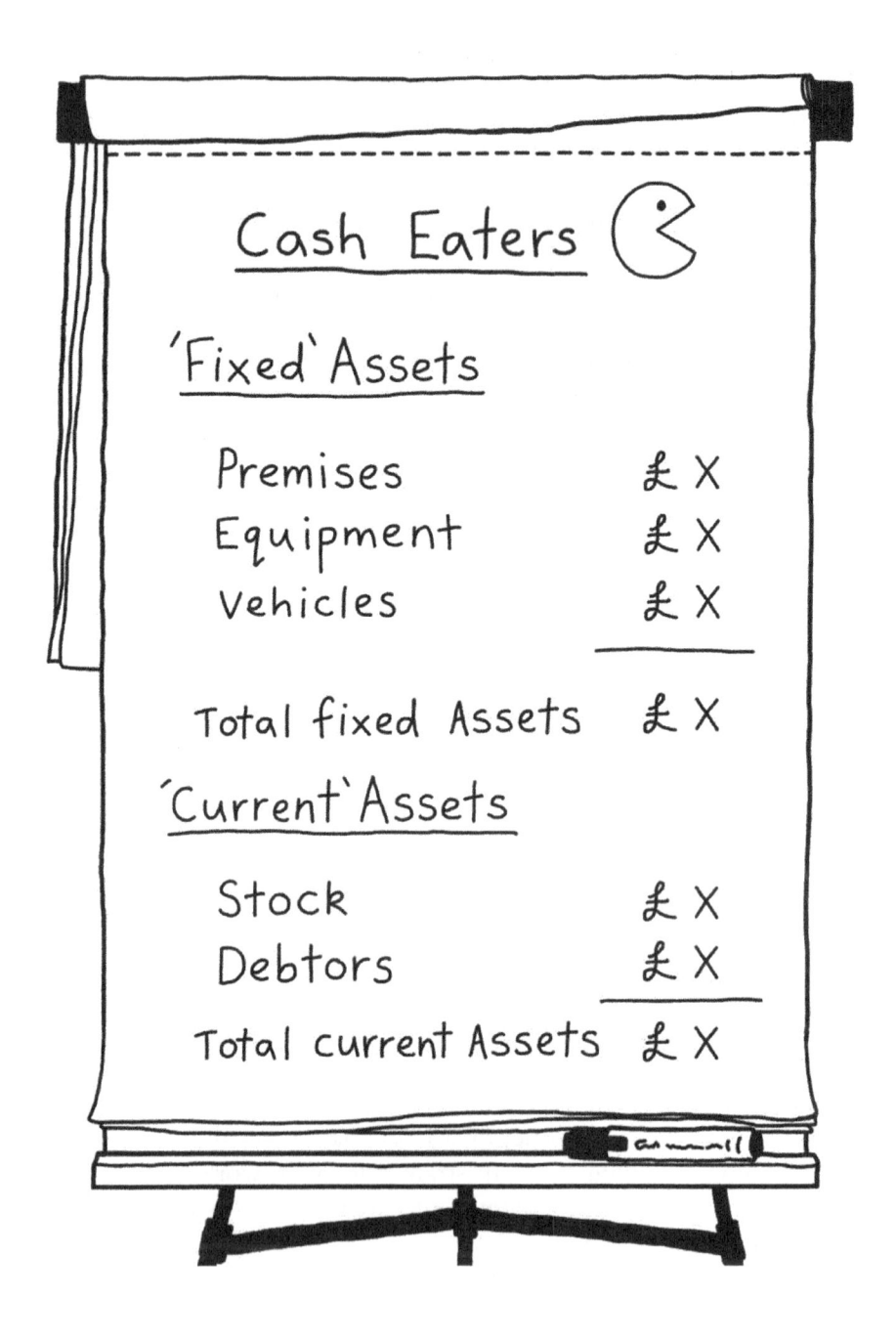

'Fixed' Assets

Premises	£ X
Equipment	£ X
Vehicles	£ X
Total fixed Assets	£ X

'Current' Assets

Stock	£ X
Debtors	£ X
Total current Assets	£ X

There can be a tendency to think that your customers are more price sensitive than they actually are. This, combined with the desire to be busy highlighted earlier, can lead you to undercharge for your work. The only way that you fill find out is by trying out different strategies and seeing what happens.

Running a business might be seen to be more of an art than a science. What route you should follow needs to be worked out using a combination of analysis and gut feel. You need to be clear about what exactly you are selling, who you are selling to, why they will value your offering and who you your competitors might be.

Being able to pay your bills on time (cash)

As mentioned earlier not having the cash to be able to pay your bills on time is as likely to bring about business failure as not being profitable. So where might cash get tied up in business and what things might cause cash problems?

To run a business, you need resources or assets. As we did when we looked at the different costs of running a business the different kinds of assets required to run your business can be split into two groups; fixed assets, which don't tend to vary in line with turnover and so called current assets, which do fluctuate as sales go up and down. Commonly to start a business you will need some form of premises to work from, some equipment and some form of transport. These will all be examples of fixed assets i.e. they don't change that much with how busy you are. To acquire the use of these assets requires cash. That cash will be tied up in the asset until it is no longer required and sold. It is the same as buying your house; to buy your house you need cash, some may be your own money from savings the rest by way of a mortgage; that cash will be tied up in the house until it is sold.

When you start trading, cash will also be caught up in stock (if you are making or selling goods) and debtors (money that is owed to you from customers). These are examples of current assets i.e. the amount of cash tied up here varies on an almost daily basis. If you are involved in the manufacture of goods then your stock might comprise of a combination of raw materials, work in progress and finished goods ready for sale. It is also interesting to note in service based industries that cash can get tied up in work in progress. This would be the money that you have had to invest in projects which has yet to be invoiced to the customer.

Cash – The 'fuel' required to run your business

The faster you drive it the more fuel it needs

The bigger the car the more fuel it needs

The worse it is maintained the more fuel it will use

"If you run out of fuel you are stuffed!"

The cash that is tied up in the day to day trading of the business is often called the Working Capital of the business. This trading cash position can be helped by receiving credit from your suppliers hence the term creditors (people you owe money to). The amount of cash tied up at any given time can simply be worked out as follows: -

Working Capital = Stock + Debtors – Creditors

The amount of cash tied up in these areas will vary from day to day but over time you will often see patterns of highs and lows in the cash requirement of a business. Working out where these peak requirements of cash is of critical importance to the viability of the business i.e. you must have the appropriate funding in place to cover the peak amounts.

An analogy for understanding the importance of cash within a business is that cash is like the fuel that we require to run a car. The bigger the car (business) is the more fuel it requires, the faster we drive the car (grow the business) the more fuel it requires and the worse we are at looking after the car (managing the business) the more fuel it requires as it runs less efficiently. To put it plainly, 'If you run out of fuel you are stuffed!!'

Four ways your working capital will change
The next business essentials rule is that there are four ways that the amount of cash tied up in the working capital of your business will change: -

    1. Increase or decrease in the volume of sales

If all your trading terms remain the same the working capital requirement of a business will vary directly in line with changes in sales e.g. if you increased sales by 50% you would expect to need 50% more stock, have 50% more debtors and receive 50% more credit. If you already had £100k tied up in working capital this would increase this figure by 50% i.e. you would have to find another £50k from somewhere to fund your business.

    2. Changes in trading terms

Changes in how long you are willing to give your customers to pay, or in the credit you receive from your suppliers, will either worsen or improve your cash position.

    3. How effectively you manage your business

Many businesses, because they fail to understand the importance of cash, are poor in managing the day to day cash position of the business. This might include not invoicing clients on time, failing to agree stage payments

$ Cash Suppliers €

1) Owners money

2) Profits retained

3) Sell something

4) Borrow it

on larger contracts, errors in paperwork, not chasing customers for payment or holding too much stock. One business that I worked with, on doing an audit of why customers were paying them late, found that in over 80% of cases this had been caused by internal issues i.e. their mistake! The less effectively you manage your business the more cash it will eat up.

    4. Seasonal trading

Most businesses will have an element of seasonal trading i.e. times when they are busier than others. This leads to peaks in the cash requirement of the business at certain points of the year.

Four places to fund your business

'Show me the money!' This is not just a great line from the film Jerry Maguire but a critical issue when running your business. We have seen how cash can get tied up in both the long and short term within your business. All this cash must come from somewhere. This leads us to our next business essentials rule; there are only four places to get the cash to fund your business. These are: -

    1. The business owner's own money

This could be personal savings for a sole trader/partnership or issuing share capital for a limited company or PLC.

    2. Retain profits within the business

Profits are not just about making someone rich. Generating profits and using them to fund the replacement/addition of assets or for funding future growth is critical for any business; even if you are running a social enterprise run on a 'not only for profits' basis.

    3. Sell something to release the cash

Whilst selling an asset might release cash, this can only work if the asset is no longer needed within your business. It might be shooting yourself in the foot to sell your car to pay your suppliers and then to have no way of travelling to your next job!

    4. Borrowing

For example, loans, overdraft, HP, invoice factoring etc.

Overtrading

A cash problem that can sneak up to scupper a fast growing business is called overtrading. Overtrading is when a business grows faster than it has the assets or capability to support. It can lead to the business going bust. When this is a cash problem it happens when the rapid growth ties up more

An Outbreak of Common Sense

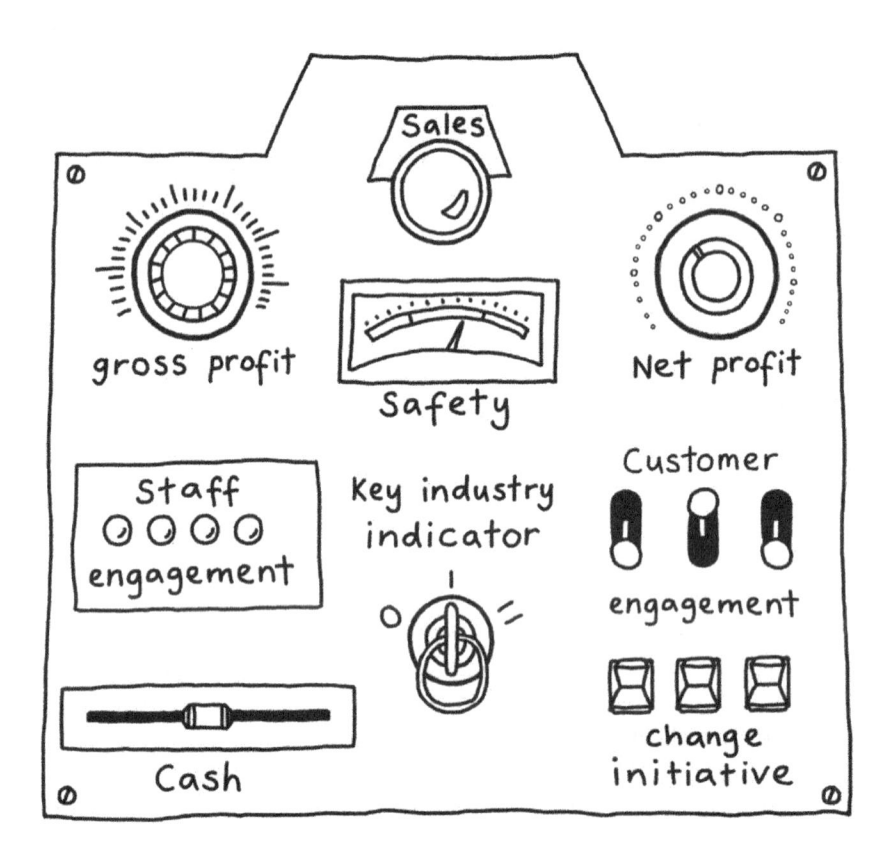

Business control Panel

Illustration of a business control panel with the following labeled components: gross profit (dial), Sales (dial), Net profit (dial), Safety (gauge), Staff engagement (four indicators), Key industry indicator (key switch), Customer engagement (three toggle switches), Cash (slider), change initiative (three buttons).

and more cash in stock and debtors eventually exhausting all available funding options. The business owner is often oblivious of this until it becomes too late as they get caught up in the 'success' of an ever growing order book.

The cash strapped owners rarely have any more money available to put into the business themselves, there isn't enough time to turn profits into cash and selling something is likely to have a detrimental impact on business operations. This means that they are forced to try and borrow the money. We have seen from the turbulent financial times over recent years this support is not always forthcoming.

The Business Control Panel
If you are going to get your people to be more commercially minded, you must have a way of letting them know how the business is doing. We play any game with more intensity if we are keeping score; the same is true in business. For people to be truly involved in the 'game' of business, they need to know how what they are doing is affecting overall performance. People pay most attention to what is being measured. If they don't have regular sight of the bottom line they won't do anything about it. You could try shouting 'motivating' comments at them like, 'Do more!', 'Work harder!' or 'That was great but we have got to do even more next year!' I don't know about you, but when someone speaks to me like that I am very tempted to tell them what they can do with their game!

But many businesses are run this way. Information about the bottom line performance of the business is held by a selected few senior people. Each month this elite group will pore over the business results and then tell people that they must do more or do better. I worked with one business which had made a significant loss in the previous year. This was whilst having a full order book and the people in the workshop operating flat out all year. The management hadn't shared the financial information with the workforce throughout the year as they thought news of the growing losses would demoralise staff. There was near uproar when people found out after the year end. They thought that because they had been busy then they must have been successful. If key information had been shared earlier then everyone could have worked together to turn the position around.

Whilst there are clearly some sensitivities that need to be observed in how financial information is shared within your business, I believe that everyone should have sight of a 'business control panel' each month to see how things are progressing. This should include as a minimum; sales (year to date), gross profit, net profit, debtors, stock, creditors, annual comparisons,

Business Essentials
Business basics in a nutshell

A successful business must do 2 things

- **Have more money coming in than going out** (Profit)
- **Pay its bills on time** (Cash)

Simple P&L
Sales - Variable Costs = Gross Profit
Gross Profit – Fixed Costs = Net Profit

Cash Eaters
Fixed – equipment, vehicles, premises
Working cash – Stock, WIP, Debtors

4 Ways to increase profit
1) Sell more 2) Costs down
3) Prices up 4) Change mix

4 Changes in working cash
1) Turnover up/down 2) Change terms
3) Seasonal up/down 4) Management

4 Cash Sources
1) Owners money 2) Retain profits
3) Sell something 4) Borrow it

approximate forecasts for the remainder of the year. In addition to this, your business control panel could include information about other key parts of your business e.g. safety performance, staff engagement, customer engagement, progress on a change initiative etc. All this information should be prepared in a simple to read, accessible form, preferably summarised on one sheet of paper.

You should use your business control panel in the same way that a pilot would use their instrument panel when flying a plane. The pilot has various dials/indicators on their control panel. The bigger, more prominent the dial the more important the thing is e.g. direction, height, speed, fuel, altitude etc. When the pilot looks at the dials the question they are working to is, 'Was that what I expected to see?' For example, if they could see that their wings weren't level but they were turning the plane, they wouldn't be worried. But if they were expecting the wings to be level they would quickly do further investigations to find out why. The same thing is true when you are 'flying' or running a business. The key performance data on your business control panel helps you to see if everything is progressing as you think it should be. If something is out of line with expectations, then it will prompt further investigation and corrective action.

When we introduced the core business essentials concepts of profit and cash (see the business essentials checklist over) to the operations functions of a large oil and gas engineering company there was a dramatic improvement in the bottom line performance of the business. Up until then production staff had defined success primarily as getting the job completed on time and within budget. Post the workshops they reviewed stock ordering and management processes, worked with the finance team to chase payments to ensure the invoicing system was as effective as possible and reviewed how they priced jobs. This included the idea of varying their pricing dependant on the perceived value of the work to the client.

Running a successful business really isn't rocket science. The key is ensuring everyone understands the basics about profit and cash and then applies this to everything that they are doing.

Ideas for action
Improve the profitability of your business
Think of one thing that you could do right now to improve the profitability of your business. Remember the four ways you can increase your profit as you think about this.
- Sell more – What could you do to bring more business in?
- Costs down – What is one thing you could do to reduce costs or improve the efficiency of your business?
- Prices up – Consider the last time you reviewed your prices. Where is one area of your business where it might be ok to test how price sensitive your market is by increasing your prices?
- Change your mix – What could you add to your business? What might you need to stop doing to focus more on your core offering?

Review the cash position of your business
On a scrap of paper, work out rough figures for your business in these three areas: -
- How much do your customers owe you? (Debtors)
- How much stock or uninvoiced work have you got? (Stock)
- How much money do you owe to other people, excluding borrowing? (Creditors)

Work out your working capital requirement by adding the figures for debtors and stock together and take off the figure for creditors. Consider the following questions: -
- How much might this figure increase by at the busiest time of your year?
- How much do you hope to grow your business by this year? Increase your working capital figure by the same percentage you expect to grow your business by.
- Where will you find the cash to cover any increase in your working capital?
- What could you do to get your money in quicker?
- What could you do to reduce the amount of stock or work in progress you have?

Personal challenges
If you have access to the financial information, find an appropriate way to share this monthly with a wider group. If you don't have access to the financial information, within the next 4 weeks, work out who you need to ask and prepare a case for why you want to regularly see this information.

Business essentials summary

- To run a successful business, you need to: -
    - have more money coming in than going out (profit)
    - be able to pay your bills on time (cash)
- There are for ways to increase the profit of a business: -
    - Sell more
    - Increase prices
    - Reduce costs
    - Change the mix of what you sell
- Cash is tied up in your business assets
    - The working capital requirement of a business is
  Stock (including Work in Progress) + Debtors – Creditors
- Working capital requirement may vary in four ways: -
    - Increase/decrease in turnover
    - Changes in trading terms
    - Effectiveness in managing your business
    - Seasonal trading
- There are four places to get the cash required to run a business
    - Owners money
    - Borrow it
    - Retain profits
    - Sell something
- If you run out of cash, you are stuffed!
- Everyone has a part to play in enhancing the profit and cash positions of an organisation. People need to understand the business essentials and then apply them to everything they do.
- You need to create a clear Business Control Panel so that everyone can be part of the game.

Chapter 3
Trust

The greater the trust, the better the organisation

'Ok, so what did you learn about trust on your team building event?'

'What the heck am I doing here?!'

The thought cannoned around my head. I was clinging precariously to a rocky outcrop about 300 feet up, on what felt like, a sheer cliff in the heart of the English Lake District. 'Does anyone fancy coming for a walk in the fells today?' had been the question my manager, Andy, had cheerfully asked us all about three hours previously.

I was working at a training and development centre which had its roots in outdoor experiential learning. How I had got the job I don't know as when they had asked me if I liked outdoor activities, I had told them that I didn't mind the odd game of golf. It didn't seem to impress a great deal!

Now whilst I don't mind a walk in the country I really don't like

49

An Outbreak of Common Sense

heights. My motto had always been to avoid the 'sharp and pointy' bits of mountains. I had find the view at the top is just as good if you choose to go up the easy way!

'Where are you going?' I had asked knowing that I was now in the esteemed company of some highly qualified outdoor types.

'Oh, just for a gentle stroll in the hills on a beautiful crisp January day. The sheep use this area all the time,' he had confidently replied.

I should have been more suspicious when I saw him loading ropes, harnesses and ice axes into the minibus. Now here I was, watching a rope snake up the mountain as Andy navigated his way up the next pitch of our 'walk in the fells', wondering what sheep used this area unless they came to commit suicide!

I was at the extreme edge of what I believed that I was capable of, maybe not physically but definitely mentally. Andy though had seen something different in me. He knew that I was up to the challenge this particular scramble posed. We were using a technique that I believe was called Alpine short roping. This involves being roped together with your partner and working your way up through a series of short stages. The lead climber finds a safe position to belay the following climber up each stage, offering them protection if they fall.

As the 'walk' progressed I gradually became more confident. I could see that the climbing wasn't beyond my capability and as I watched Andy comfortably and confidently lead each stage I felt sure that I could trust him with my safety if I did slip up. I am not saying that I got to enjoying myself but I did manage at least to appreciate the amazing view of the Lakes that this vantage point offered.

Whilst my day in the fells won't ever register in the annals of the mountaineering greats, I would never have managed to achieve this challenge on my own. It was only made possible by trusting both Andy's assessment of my capabilities and his rock climbing skills. One question though did come to mind as we strolled down the gentler, sheep filled slopes on the far side of the fell.

'Andy? What would have happened if you had fallen?'

His reply will stay with me forever.

'Well then we would have both been f***ed!!'

When trust is lost

I once worked with an IT department of a large insurance company that had recently gone through a major reorganisation. Because of this upheaval every department and business unit within the company wanted the support of the IT department to resolve their particular issues. The IT department soon became overwhelmed by the demand for their services.

As the situation continued individuals within the department became increasingly stressed and moved to more defensive positions, just trying to look after themselves. Internal relations started to break down as people perceived each other as being uncaring and somewhat 'economical with the truth' in how they were communicating the state of various individual projects.

During the workshop, we explored the issues of trust in action within a team exercise based on the 'prisoners' dilemma'. This forces teams to consider how they should balance self-interest with the needs of the whole group. Within the exercise, they unanimously adopted a position of high mutual trust and collaborative working. This was the only time I have seen a group do this in this exercise.

When we debriefed the exercise the group remarked that the positive way that they had approached the exercise was nothing like the toxic atmosphere that pervaded their department back at work.

These people clearly wanted to do the right thing but under pressure resorted to less positive behaviours and thereby created a downward spiral of in-fighting and a low trust culture. Sadly, for those involved the situation got so bad that the company saw the only way to resolve the issue was to outsource the whole operation.

The need for trust

Life is about relationships. From the earliest of days people have understood that we have the best chance of surviving and thriving if we work cooperatively with others; we can achieve more, our emotional and physical needs are more likely to be met and our weaknesses can be offset by other's strengths. It is plain common sense that the stronger our relationships, the greater the chances are that our needs will be met. This is true in any social group you might like to define; families, friends, clubs, work, businesses etc.

At the heart of any relationship is trust. The greater the levels of trust the better the relationship will be. One analogy that can be used is that trust is the oil that lubricates relationships. People are all different. Sometimes we find people we fit well with and other times, no matter what we do, we seem to rub each other up the wrong way. The greater the levels of trust between people the more likely they are to work harmoniously together and minimise the friction of personal differences. Just think for a moment what it is like: -

- to work in a team where there are low levels of trust
- to be in a business without trusting relationships with customers, suppliers or staff
- to be in a relationship with a partner where trust has been lost or damaged.

Where there are low levels of trust huge amounts of energy are wasted in game playing and politics. Trust ultimately underpins our wellbeing and our effectiveness, either individually or in groups. An example of what can happen when trust is lost in an organisation is seen in the story over the page.

What is trust?

Trust is a belief. It is a belief that someone or something can and will deliver if we put our faith in them.

Trust is an action. Whether we truly trust someone or something is only evident in our actions. It means taking a risk, leaving ourselves exposed to undesirable consequences if what we are trusting fails to deliver.

During my time at the outdoor development organisation we used high rope activities as part of the development offering. This gave delegates a real opportunity to explore the nature of trust in action. Under supervision from a qualified technician, your safety during a given exercise was placed into the hands of your colleagues. It was a very different thing whilst

The 'Universal' Principles

1) **Caring**
   You care about the other party's interests

2) **Honesty**
   You are truthful in your dealings

3) **Fairness**
   You treat others fairly

you were still on the ground to say that you trusted your mates, from leaping of the top of a 30-foot-high pole into thin air with only a harness, a clip and what seemed like a very thin rope to support you! Trust only happens when you take that leap of faith and rely on someone else to deliver.

Trust is primarily a subconscious decision. Clearly, we shouldn't trust lightly. If you are taking a risk you should have a good basis on which to do this. Whether we believe we should trust someone or not is based on a predominately subconscious assessment of two areas; do I believe that this person can do this thing and do I believe that they will do this thing.

We know if we trust someone or something through a feeling. It is almost like a kinaesthetic set of traffic lights in our gut. If your gut feeling is good you trust, if not, you don't. This feeling comes from the subconscious interpretation of hundreds of external signals running through a filter of past experiences and beliefs. This is an extremely complex process that can be performed in the fraction of a second! These signals might be tiny e.g. a slight narrowing of the eyes, looking away or a flaring of the nostrils. These signals are often too subtle to pick up consciously.

Trust is linked to the core human driver of self-preservation. This can often put us in the difficult situation of wanting to trust someone but not being able to let go in practice as the risks feel too great. (See later chapter 'The three reasons why I don't delegate')

The earlier example about doing a high ropes activity gives a graphic illustration of the conscious/subconscious dialogue of trust in action. Our conscious is a bit like listening to BBC Radio 4, very logical and reasoned. It says things like, 'They wouldn't get you to do this if it wasn't safe. No one is going to drop you. They have done this exercise thousands of times.' Meanwhile your subconscious is screaming inside your head like some mad 1960s pirate radio station on full volume saying, 'Don't do it! You're going to die!'

The 'Universal' Principles

Both your own and your organisation's long term success are underpinned by you living by three core principles; caring, honesty and fairness. These principles are I believe universal in that they are applicable in any time or culture, anywhere in the world. Do you care about me and my interests? Are you being honest with me? Will you treat me fairly? The universal nature of these principles can be seen in how often you see them cropping up in the values statements of organisations. Stating values though is a lot

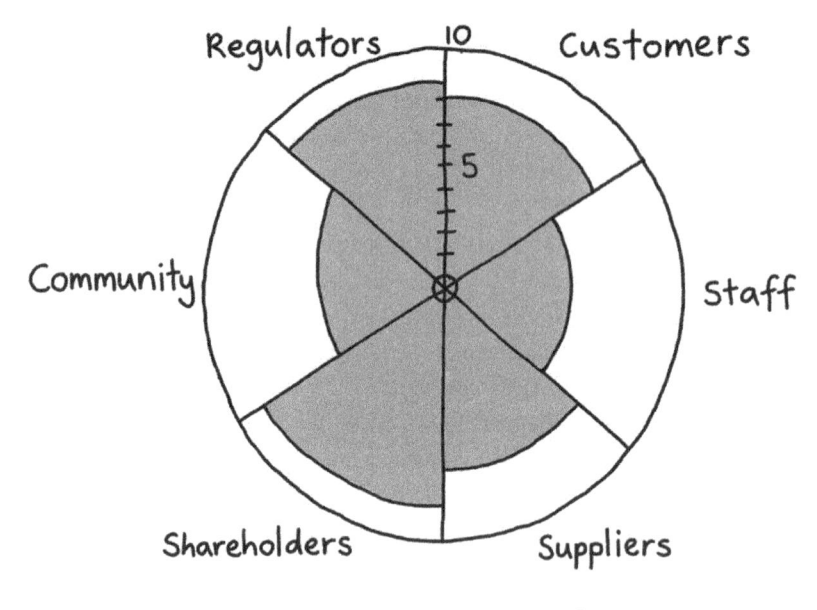

Trust Wheel

easier than living by them. Stepping outside of the universal principles will cause you problems. If you believe that someone has dealt with you in an uncaring, dishonest or unfair way you will either walk away from the relationship or seek to redress the balance in some way. Let's look at how different groups might respond if they believe any of these principles might have been broken.

Customers – Complaint levels will rise. Customers will become more demanding. Individuals will seek to mobilise other disgruntled customers using social media tools to bring pressure on the organisation. They may delay payment of invoices. Ultimately, they will take their business elsewhere.

Staff – Initially staff might withdraw any discretionary effort. They will work to rule, only doing the minimum of what is asked of them. You will see an increase in the levels of poor time keeping and sickness as people look to redress the 'wrong' they think has been done to them. Productivity and quality levels will fall as staff become disengaged and care less. Ultimately you will see increases in unwanted staff turnover as people vote with their feet and leave.

Suppliers – The most common way that suppliers feel that the universal principles have been breached is through late payment of their invoices. It seems to be accepted 'good business practice' to delay paying your bills for as long as possible. However, the more you do this the more the frustrated supplier will seek to even the score. They will become inflexible in how they supply you. They will seek to raise their prices. They also may seek to lobby other suppliers to take group action against a larger customer. They will withdraw credit terms. Ultimately, they will refuse to supply you.

If you breach any of the universal principles it will come back to bite you at some point. The relationship of trust is critical to the efficiency and effectiveness of your organisation. You can use the 'Trust Wheel' over the page to rate your perceptions of the quality of the trust relationship with all your key stakeholders. Any low score will make for a bumpy ride!

It is important to note here that what matters is not whether you think that you have been caring, honest and fair in your actions but whether the other person perceives your actions this way. You may infer how people perceive your actions by observing how they react to you but the only way that you are going to really know is by asking them. You should continually look for feedback from all stakeholders/interested parties as to how they

Capability ↑ | limit of your capability

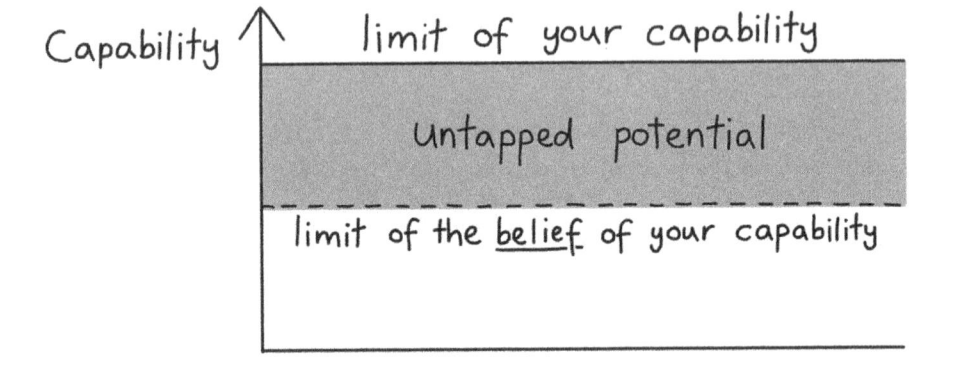

untapped potential

limit of the <u>belief</u> of your capability

perceive your actions and the quality of your relationship. Questions you might ask customers or suppliers include: -
- Do you think we live by our stated values?
- Do we demonstrate care for you and your organisation?
- Do you perceive us to be honest in our dealings with you?
- Are we fair in how we deal with you?

It is my belief that in recent times we have lost sight of the importance of the universal principles of caring, honesty and fairness. One only has to look at the global banking crisis in 2008 to see the danger of what happens when self-interest, greed and dishonesty become institutionally acceptable. Living by universal principles is not just the right thing to do ethically but it is the right thing to do to ensure the long term performance of your organisation.

Trusting yourself

Trust is not just about trusting others but also about trusting yourself. Trusting yourself is also strongly linked to your safety/self-preservation driver. It might not be politically correct to say this but we all have limited capabilities. I'm not a fan of statements like, 'anything is possible if you believe it'. Those of you who will have seen my somewhat rotund physique will know that I certainly couldn't run the 100m in under 10 seconds, no matter how much I wanted to believe it!

Our personal effectiveness is governed by an accurate assessment of our capabilities. If we get ourselves into situations that are beyond our capabilities, we are likely to put ourselves at risk. However, if we underestimate our capabilities we will not fulfil our full potential.

To keep ourselves safe we tend to underestimate our capabilities (see figure over). This is why others often see more potential in us than we see in ourselves. Self-doubt is not actually a bad thing. It seeks to keep you safe but if overplayed it will limit your potential. If we are to achieve more, we continually need to test the boundaries of our perceived capabilities. We need to ask ourselves the question, 'Is this the limit of my perceived capability or my actual capability?' This is often best achieved through a series of small steps, taking on incremental new challenges, reviewing them and building self-confidence and self-trust.

Ideas for Action
Trust reflection
For each member of your team consider the following questions: -
- On a scale of 1-10, how would you rate the quality of your relationship?
- In what areas do you really trust them?
- In what areas might you have some reservations?
- What is the basis for your judgements?
- What would be the first thing that would need to happen to enhance your relationship?

Trust wheel
Complete the trust wheel exercise for your organisation or department. Choose appropriate labels for all the key stakeholders (groups who have a vested interest in the success of your organisation).
- What are your reflections on your wheel?
- What would you have to do to create a 'smoother ride' and enhance areas of lower trust?

Personal challenges
Use the 5 questions from the trust reflection above to make a short feedback questionnaire. Ask members of your team to complete the questionnaire to give you feedback on the quality of your relationship. (You may want to use an online survey tool such as Survey Monkey or ask a 3rd party to collate people's responses to preserve anonymity)
Health warning – This exercise should be carried out with care and sensitivity. Respect people's feedback and reflect on it. Don't seek to justify your actions.

Ask three people, whose opinion you trust, to identify 2 or 3 areas where you have potential that is as yet untapped.
- What would it take for you to use this potential?
- What could you do to test the boundaries of your potential?
- What risks are you prepared to take?
- What support might you find helpful?

Summary of Trust
- Life is about relationships. The better our relationships are the more effective we will be.
- Trust is at the heart of relationships. The more trust there is the better relationships will be.
- Trust is a belief, a belief that someone can and will deliver if you take the risk
- Assessment of trust is done subconsciously. We know if we trust someone or not through a gut feeling
- The 'universal principles' that underpin all relationships are care, honesty and fairness. If people perceive that they have been treated in a way that is uncaring, dishonest or unfair it will come back to bite you.
- 'Universal principles' of care, honesty and fairness are both ethically right as well as the right thing to enhance your organisation's performance.
- Our untapped potential lies in the gap between the limits of the belief of our capability and the actual limit of our capability.
- Self-doubt is not a bad thing as it keeps you safe however we need to continually challenge ourselves to access untapped potential

Chapter 4
Create Partners

The more engaged your people are and the more they are encouraged to use their initiative, the more effective your organisation will be

I was recently working with a construction company and got caught up in a 'healthy debate' with one of the directors about the idea of creating 'partners' in his business; staff who are so invested in the business that they see it as their own. He maintained that the idea of having highly engaged staff who were encouraged to use their initiative was ok for his managers but completely irrelevant for the manual labourers within his business. He wasn't going to budge from his position until one of his site foremen offered his view.

One of his labourers had recently dug through a water main whilst preparing the foundations for a building and had caused many thousands of pounds of damage. The labourer had seen the water main but continued to dig the hole. He had assumed that it was ok because that is what he had been told to do! Which labourer would you want? One who just did what he was told or one that saw the problem and used their initiative to check if

An Outbreak of Common Sense

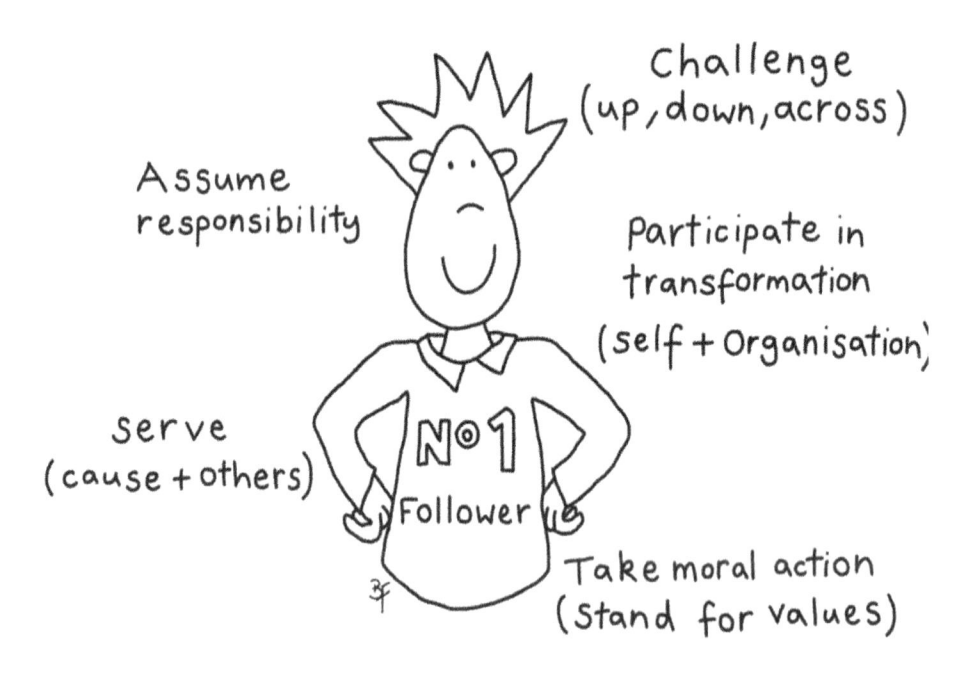

Challenge
(up, down, across)

Assume
responsibility

Participate in
transformation
(self + Organisation)

Serve
(cause + others)

N° 1
Follower

Take moral action
(Stand for values)

they should continue digging? The site foreman certainly knew and the director got the point!

One place where there has been a shift in the thinking about leadership and followership is the military. Military organisations were built around a simple idea. Senior officers did the 'thinking', the rank and file soldiers did what they were told! This principle worked fine whilst the officers could see and understand the unfolding battle and when both armies were playing by the same 'rules'. However, the world changed. The opposition stopped playing by the rules, battles moved from being set piece engagements to short skirmishes, often within civilian areas, and any target became fair game. Against this backdrop the old military model became useless. It was too slow and cumbersome to react to the fast changing situation. By the time soldiers on the ground got orders from their officers they were either dead or the enemy had gone.

The military model has had to change. Troops on the ground now must be able to use their initiative to decide how best to deal with the situation that they face. Senior officers, still retain overall authority, but this now needs to be exercised in setting overall objectives, mission parameters and principles of engagement for the troops to work within. This has been a challenging transition for military organisations where traditional command and control leadership prevailed, but a change that was essential if they were to remain effective in a fast changing world.

Many modern day organisations are trapped in the old military approach; 'thinking' is done by leaders and 'doing' is done by workers. This is all well and good if your world is relatively predictable and stable. If though, like the army, your organisation is facing a world of change you need to rethink what you need from your 'leaders' and 'troops'. Ira Chaleff, in his excellent book 'The Courageous Follower', looks at one half of this challenge when he describes 5 key attributes of an excellent team member or 'follower'. These are; they assume responsibility, they serve, they are prepared to challenge, they participate in transformation and they take moral action. The first two of these attributes speak of engagement; the other three attributes reflect initiative. The more people like that we have in our teams the greater the chance we will have of being successful.

So, let's for a moment look at the two areas or engagement and initiative, consider what type of 'followers' you might have and explore how this might be impacting the effectiveness of your organisation.

An Outbreak of Common Sense

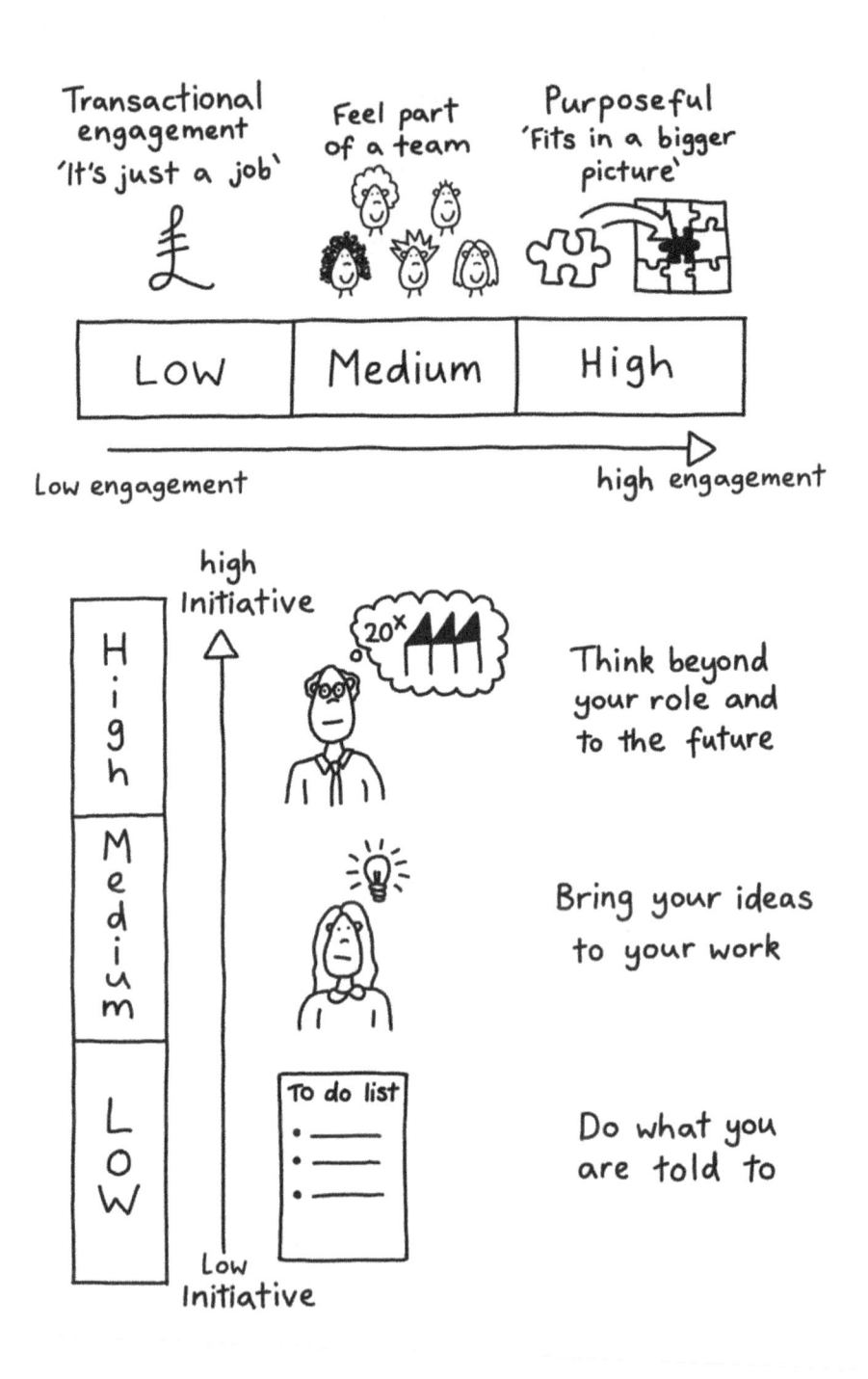

Transactional engagement 'It's just a job'	Feel part of a team	Purposeful 'Fits in a bigger picture'
Low	Medium	High

Low engagement → high engagement

High Initiative

High — Think beyond your role and to the future

Medium — Bring your ideas to your work

Low — Do what you are told to

Low Initiative

66

Engagement

The level of people's engagement will vary over time. This being said, you often see people settling into a certain level of engagement with their organisation.

People who have low levels of engagement will have a transactional relationship with the organisation. If this is their paid work, then they will see their role in the organisation just as a job. As levels of engagement increase people have a broader sense of connection with the organisation, this is commonly linked to people feeling part of a team or wider group. At the highest levels of engagement people will have a strong sense of purpose in their work; what they do matters.

One of the clearest indicators of people's level of engagement is in the language that they use. If engagement levels are low, you will hear people use 'you, your or they' e.g. 'I work for you or your organisation. They don't understand me.' As levels of engagement increase people 'own' their organisation more and will increasingly use words like 'we and our' in their language.

Initiative

As with engagement the amount of initiative people are prepared to use in their work will vary over time but patterns of behaviour often develop.

With low levels of initiative people generally only do what they are told to do. As levels of initiative grow, people start bringing their ideas and thinking to their work and are willing to take increased levels of responsibility. At the highest levels of initiative people will apply their thinking, beyond their role, to the wider organisation's performance, taking a big picture view. In this they demonstrate a concern for the future direction and health of the organisation.

The two areas of engagement and initiative are linked. The more engaged people are, the more they will bring their thinking to what they are doing. The more they are encouraged to bring their initiative to their work, the more engaged they will be. Of course, this can also work in reverse! Where a person might be at any given time in these two areas will lead them to being one of four broad types of team member or follower; Resources – (Low engagement/Low initiative), Protestors – (Low engagement/High initiative), Conformists – (High engagement/Low initiative) and Partners – (High engagement/High initiative)

An Outbreak of Common Sense

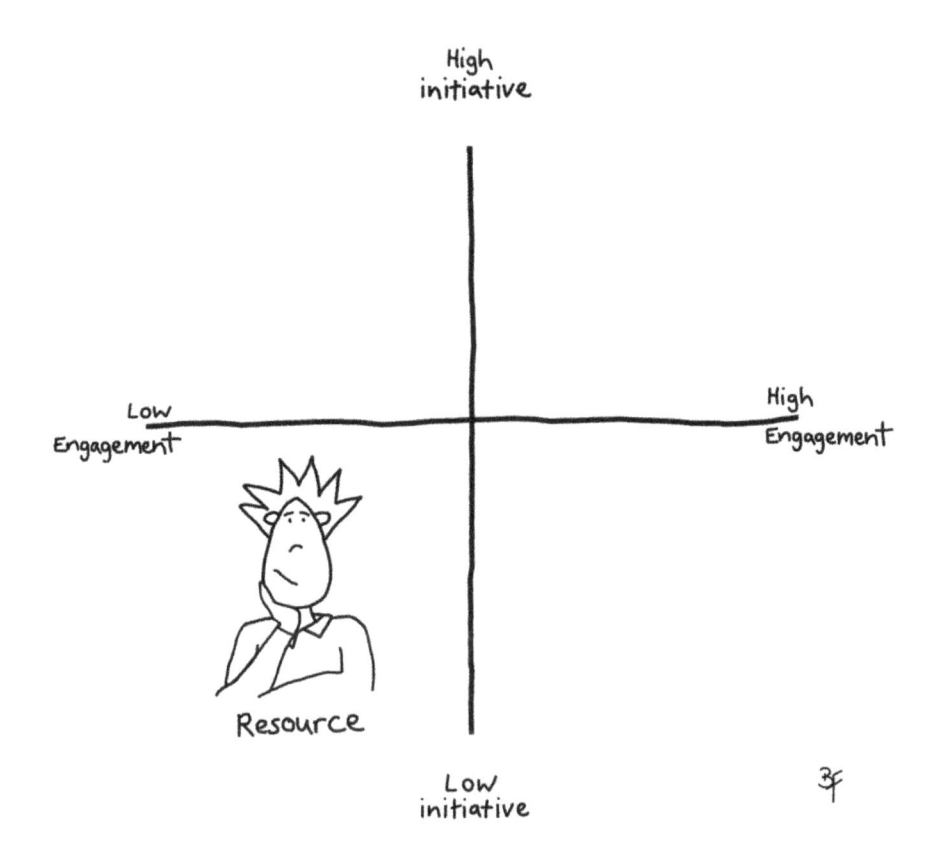

High initiative

Low Engagement — High Engagement

Resource

Low initiative

Resources

A Resource type follower is a member of staff who is relatively disengaged with the organisation and brings very little initiative to their work. They will do the minimum that they must do and no more. Their approach to work might be described as follows: -

- I see work to pay the bills
- I only do what I am paid to do
- I work for the money
- I believe that it is the manager's job to come up with ideas as to how to improve things
- It is my job to do, not to ask
- I feel resigned to the job I do
- It's only a job
- I see myself as just a cog in a large machine

Many managers that I have worked with say that they like the idea of having some Resource type members of staff in their team. The Resource makes little fuss, often just seeking the quiet life, to do the job and to take the money. This may be fine in the short term and if things remain the same. However, issues occur when things start happening that require staff to be more flexible or to respond to something that might fall outside of their immediate job description. Now the 'jobsworth', inflexible attitude and approach of the Resource quickly has a detrimental effect on the performance of the organisation as things fail to get done that fall outside of their defined role.

If you have Resource type followers in your team you will continually have to monitor what is happening and step in to give instruction. This is extremely time consuming and may well lead you to neglect less urgent but important proactive tasks associated with being an effective manager or leader.

Turning around a Resource type follower will require you to make a concerted effort to increase their levels of engagement and in encouraging them to use their initiative more. I will explore approaches to do this later in the chapter. However, I would emphasise at this point that the most likely reason that someone has turned into a Resource is down to how they have been managed in the past. If they have been in your team for some time, you should reflect on your own management approach and consider what you are doing that is leading them to be like this.

An Outbreak of Common Sense

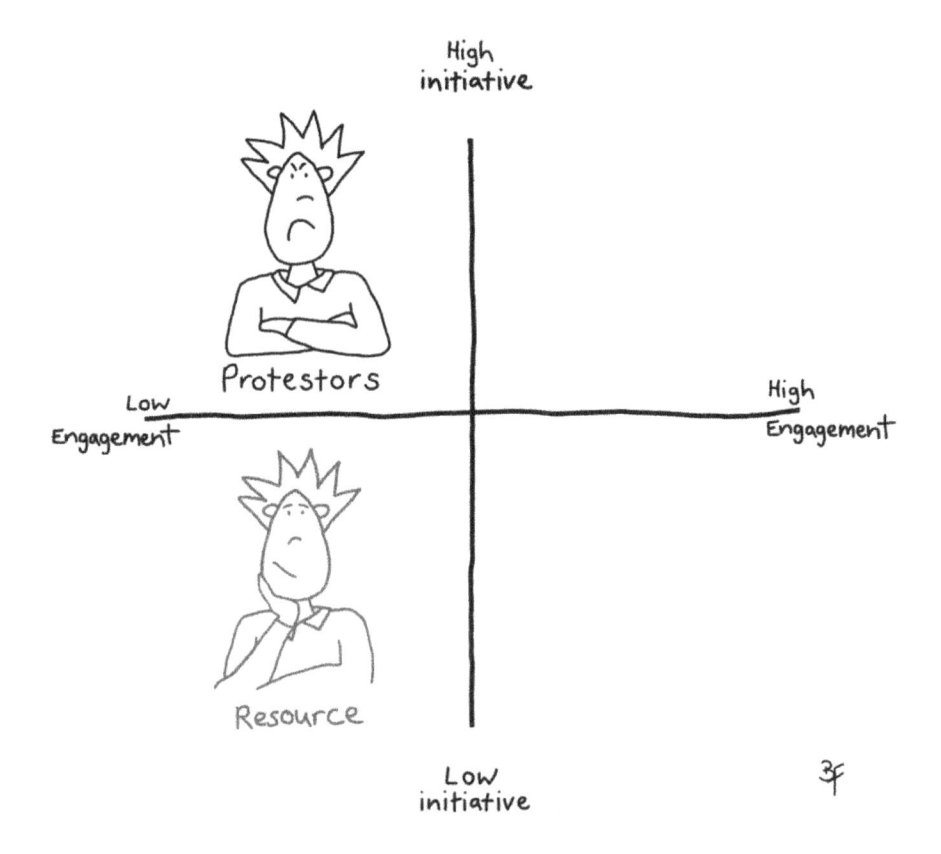

High initiative

Protestors

Low Engagement — High Engagement

Resource

Low initiative

What might you be doing that is leading them to be disengaged and discouraging them from using their initiative? You can't guarantee to change their behaviour but you can try modifying your approach to get a better outcome.

Protestors

Protestor type followers might be described as actively disengaged. Staff who fall into this category are not engaged with your agenda and use their initiative to seek to change things to their way. This might either be overt or covert resistance. Signs of being a Protestor might include: -

- I often feel frustrated with my organisation and express this
- I often find myself at odds with my leaders
- I see myself as a maverick within my organisation
- I am often sceptical about what my leaders say
- I actively seek to influence my leaders to see things differently
- I often feel that what I am trying to say is not being heard
- Whilst I will do what I am asked to do, it is often under protest
- I do the job for the money but am actively investigating alternative options

I have also met many managers who say that they would like a few Protestors in their teams as they say the challenge they offer keeps them on their toes. It must be questionable though to keep a member of staff disengaged just so they can act as a foil to you. The downsides of Protestors are easy to see. Not only do they waste their own energy, time and effort pursuing a different agenda but they are very likely to take others along with them. If you fail to address Protestors the negative effects can quickly escalate. It is almost like a cancer in an organisation; small pockets of resistance start to establish a foothold and then spread and grow 'infecting' the whole organisation.

The good news is that Protestors can be turned around and when re-engaged can become very powerful supporters of what you are seeking to achieve. At least the Protestor has something about them; they have the 'get up and go' to try to make things happen. The problem is that this is being channelled in the wrong direction.

The first thing that you need to do is to highlight the issue and bring it into the open. The behaviour of the Protestor cannot go unchecked. However, once this has been done it is important to seek to understand their position and to understand the sources of their frustration. You can

An Outbreak of Common Sense

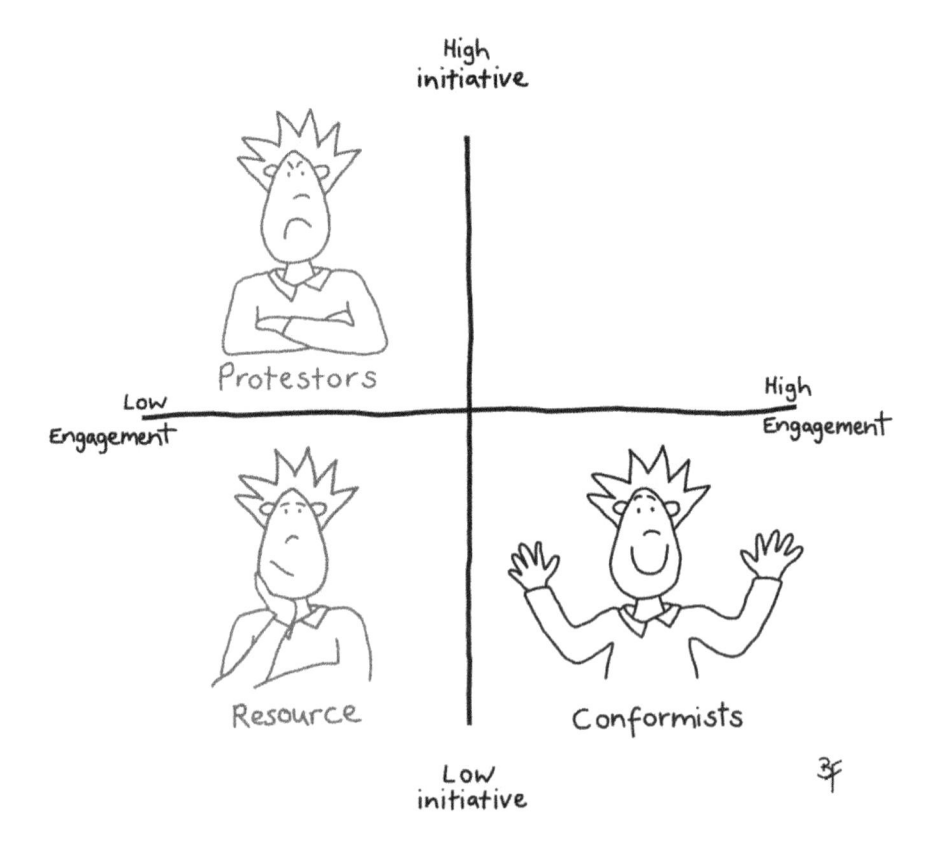

High initiative

Protestors

Low Engagement ——————|—————— High Engagement

Resource | Conformists

Low initiative

then work together to seek to find ways to address these issues and to re-engage them. I have found that making the investment in seeking to understand a Protestor's position often pays dividends. Again though, there are no guarantees of success and if it becomes clear that a positive outcome is unlikely to be achieved, it is better to agree to part ways sooner than later.

Conformists

Staff who are engaged but use very little initiative might be described as 'Conformists'. They are the eager beavers that are willing to do all that you ask but ultimately the responsibility to make things happen remains with you. A Conformist's approach to work may be described as follows: -

- I enjoy my work and am happy to do what is asked of me
- I often choose not to challenge even though I might have a different view
- I work for my boss
- I believe that I should be positive and be prepared to do whatever is asked of me
- I am happy to go along with what my leaders suggest
- I prefer my managers to make important decisions
- I am happy to go the extra mile if asked to
- I am happy to conform to others views

Sounds great you might say, just what I would want from an ideal team member! The downsides of Conformists are less obvious than the problems associated with Resources and Protestors. To highlight the issues here let me ask you a question. Do you often find that you have a lot of spare time on your hands? Chances are the answer to this will be no. With Conformists, you must do all the driving. You have to be in the detail of the day, organising and directing efforts. This is time consuming and will often mean that more strategic or complex organisational issues are not dealt with. This will have a detrimental impact on the medium to long term effectiveness of your work.

Another issue with Conformists is all the 'thinking' is left to a small number of people in the organisation. In a complex world, the chances of this small group coming up with all the best ideas is not great. Smart organisations work to the maxim, 'With every pair of hands comes a free brain, make sure you use it!'

Clearly the remedy for these issues is to get the Conformist to take

An Outbreak of Common Sense

High initiative

Protestors | Partners

Low Engagement | High Engagement

Resource | Conformists

Low initiative

more initiative. This may mean that you should look at both your approach and theirs. I highlight in the chapter 'Three reasons why we don't delegate', how we are often uncomfortable encouraging people to use their initiative more. Taking more initiative means taking more responsibility. The Conformist may not be comfortable taking the additional responsibility that goes with using their initiative more. To counter both your own and their reservations, encouraging people to take more initiative is best done through a series of small steps, building mutual confidence along the way.

Partners
Staff who are both engaged and use their initiative might be described as 'Partners'. They work with you in striving to bring about better results always looking to see how they can bring improvements to their part of the organisation. As a Partner you might display the following attributes: -

- I enjoy my work and continually seek out ways to do it better
- I actively offer ideas and suggestions for improvement
- I seek out new responsibilities and challenges
- I contribute wholeheartedly to the goals and direction of the organisation
- I bring my thinking to my work
- I work in partnership with my leader(s)
- I believe in what we are trying to do and am willing to take a stand for this
- I see my work as an integral part of my life

Effective modern organisations are built on creating 'Partner' type staff. We are facing times of unprecedented change in the world. Organisations that are succeeding are the ones that can best respond to change. The nature of work is also changing. Tasks are becoming less routine and more complex. The routine tasks, that used to be the bread and butter of large organisations, have become computerised, mechanised or outsourced. To succeed in this world, we don't need human robots, programmed to do what they have been told, instead we need engaged human beings with the ability to think on their feet. Partners will come up with the very best solution for the presenting issue.

In the past areas like staff engagement and initiative have been described as 'soft' and seen to be of secondary importance to the so called 'harder areas' of business strategies, plans, structures and systems. Not to

An Outbreak of Common Sense

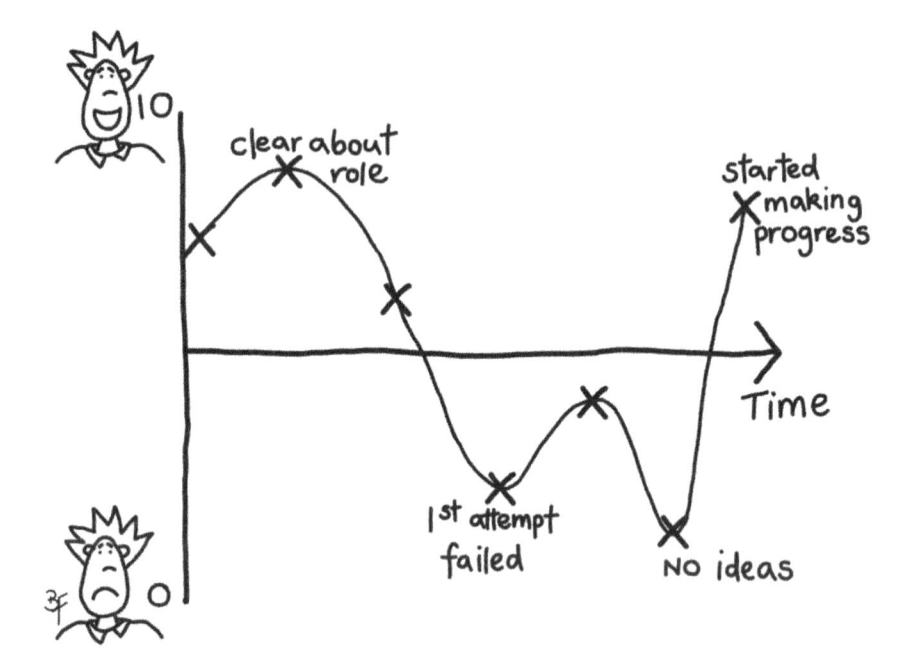

put too fine a point on it, the future success or failure of your organisation rests on getting these 'soft' areas right! So here is a challenge for you.

- If it is common sense that your organisation will be more effective if your people are engaged and bringing their initiative to their work, what are you doing to improve these two areas?
- How much of the available potential of your staff are you using – 10%, 50%, 80%? How would you know?
- How do you know how engaged your staff are on a day to day basis?
- What would need to happen to improve their levels of engagement?
- If you were to look back at the agendas for your management meetings over the last six months, how much time would have been dedicated to these two critical people issues?
- Do you focus most of your time and energy on more tangible things e.g. outputs, results, processes etc.?

The chances are that you, like most other managers and leaders, will have spent little or no time exploring how you might fundamentally enhance staff engagement or encourage your people to bring more of their thinking to their work. So, let's look at how we might be able to work with these somewhat intangible areas in a practical way.

Measuring Engagement

Staff engagement is a very difficult thing to measure. As a result, many organisations leave it to an annual or biannual survey of staff or do nothing at all. The problem is people don't readily talk about their feelings; in fact, they rarely notice how they are feeling unless they are at the extreme ends of the emotional scale. If you ask someone how they are feeling at work the standard response you are likely to hear is, 'Fine'. That 'fine' could cover anything from, 'I'm totally peed off right now' to, 'I feel really good'. Over any given period of time feelings will fluctuate, (see 'feelings chart' over), and performance will vary in line with this. It takes considerable effort to perform well and remain professional when you are feeling disengaged.

If you are going to be effective in managing engagement you need to find non-emotional ways to track and talk about feelings with your people. I have found the following three tools/frameworks helpful in doing this with a wide variety of teams.

The Engagement Checklist	
Engagement area	**Score/10**
Purpose I am clear about what we are trying to achieve and believe that this matters	
Clarity I am clear about my role, our goals and how this fits into the bigger picture	
Stretch I feel appropriately challenged in my work and believe that my potential is being fully utilised	
Appreciation I feel that what I do is valued and that this is recognised in a timely and effective way	
Inclusion I feel that I am part of a team and that what I say matters	
Fairness I am paid and treated fairly	

Feelings chart

The feelings chart is a simple tool that can be used to track how people's moods have varied over time and to explore the reasons for this. To create a feelings chart, first you draw a vertical scale. This scale varies from 0/10, 'This is awful' to 10/10, 'This is brilliant'. Next draw a horizontal line to represent the period that you want to explore. You might take an in-depth view of a short period, say a few hours, or a bigger picture overview looking at a period of days, weeks or even months. You then chart highs and lows of feeling over a given period and record what happened that led to these shifts in engagement.

You might want to try this out for yourself; it can be quite an eye opener. With a team, I get each person to draw their own feelings chart first. I then get them to share this with the whole group by drawing their line on a flipchart, getting them to talk through the highs and lows as they do so. Each team member should add their own line to the same chart using a different colour pen or line style to differentiate it. Don't worry if the chart starts to look a bit messy with all the lines on it. The amalgamation of everyone's lines helps you to see patterns in feelings, common causes and highlights individuals who have had a different experience for other reasons.

As a team exercise, ran from time to time, the feelings chart provides an excellent opportunity to talk about levels of engagement and to create individual and group actions to improve things. Anything that you can do to improve the overall level of the graphs by a few points will have a direct impact to your bottom line performance.

The Engagement Checklist

There are many factors that will affect how people are feeling at work. Six areas that have been seen to have a significant impact on engagement are Purpose, Clarity, Stretch, Appreciation, Inclusion and Fairness. Each of these areas is defined in more detail on the checklist over the page. The engagement checklist can be used as another discussion starter with your team. Each team member should rate where they are in each of the 6 areas and jot down supporting comments. You could then either explore this in a 1:1 review with each team member or run an open team session, pooling ratings and ideas. In framing these discussions it's important to highlight that you will be looking to work in partnership with your team to improve engagement and the need to focus on areas that are within your influence. It is always better to identify areas where you can achieve quick wins than

The Four Levels of Motivation

Personal Growth
Chance to develop new skills + personal growth

Connection
Feeling part of a team
Feeling part of something purposeful

Tools to do the job
Right equipment, training resources and authority to get on with the work

Basic Needs
Role clarity, Fair pay, Safety

waste time talking about an ideal wish list of potential changes that you probably can't make happen.

The Four Levels of Motivation

Another checklist that you can use in a similar way to initiate discussions with your team is based on a model called the Four Levels of Motivation. This framework draws on several different theories of motivation. Each level builds on the one below i.e. a person's motivation, and therefore engagement, builds from the bottom upwards. There is little point trying to motivate someone at a higher level if their needs have not been met at the lower levels e.g. someone is not likely to engage with your inspiring talk on the future direction and purpose of your organisation if they don't understand what their job is!

You could use this model in the same way as the engagement checklist i.e. get your team to rate each level out of 10 and then to jot down their thoughts. Alternatively, you could just use each level to prompt questions for discussion e.g.

- Do you feel safe both physically and emotionally at work e.g. no bullying, ridicule etc.?
- Are you clear about your role?
- Have you received the right levels of training/support to do your job well?
- Do you feel part of a team?
- Do you understand how what you do fits within the work of the wider organisation?
- Do you have the opportunity to learn and develop new skills?

Managing Engagement

On a 1:1 level effective management of engagement boils down to exploring three broad questions: -
  1. How are you feeling?
  2. Why are you feeling like that?
  3. What could you do to feel a bit better?

To overcome the problem of people trying to talk about their feelings it can help greatly to use scale or rating questions e.g. 'On a scale of 1-10 how are you feeling?' or in short hand, 'What number are you at?'

Initiative – How not to do it!

As part of a reorganisation in a large retail organisation it became evident that the work schedules of key departments were going to need to be changed. As a result, very well intended managers of a local store, went off into a darkened room and sweated blood and tears over the problem. They proudly emerged some days later with the new work hours for everyone. Much to their annoyance these were not well received by the team. The new hours failed to address the subtleties of the team's workload, such as quiet and busy times or when key back office work needed to be done. They also failed to address individual needs, for example flexibility around school hours for those with children.

In many ways, it was not surprising that the schedule, drawn up by the managers, failed to address these areas as they were only really known by the team members. How much more effective would it have been for the managers to go to the team and say, 'These are the parameters in which you must work e.g. budget, hours etc. Within these parameters, I want you as a team to come up with the new schedule that works best for the store and for you as individuals.'

Giving the team this choice would have engaged their thinking, tapped into their in-depth knowledge of how things worked daily and increased ownership of the new schedule. People are much more inclined to make their own ideas work than someone else's!

Traps to avoid when managing engagement
It is important to note that the third question asks what could you do to feel better not what could I do. One trap that you can fall into is to think that it is your responsibility to make people feel better. This can lead you to avoid addressing issues around engagement for fear of opening a can of worms that you might not be able to resolve.

One head teacher I worked with was trying to support a member of staff who was having issues with stress. The Head saw it as her job to dig this person out of the hole they were in. Instead of asking the member of staff what they needed to do to improve the situation for them self, she took on the responsibility of trying to make them feel better. As part of their efforts to help the Head even secured the resources to offer the troubled teacher aromatherapy sessions for relaxation. Whilst well intended the situation continued to deteriorate. By stepping in to try and rescue the teacher the Head unwittingly further undermined their self-confidence and made the situation worse.

The thinking that it is the manager's responsibility to make staff feel better can also be mirrored by staff. How many times have you seen people bemoaning how they are feeling and looking for their bosses to do something to make them feel better? Managing engagement needs to be the shared responsibility of everyone. As a manager, you continually need to be aware of the prevailing mood within your team and you need to facilitate all possible actions to improve this. This may include you taking on the responsibility for making certain things happen but should mainly involve you in helping your people to improve things for themselves. As a member of staff, you need to apply your initiative to maintain your own levels of engagement e.g. to communicate to managers where you are in terms of engagement, why you are feeling this way and what you are seeking to do to improve this.

Encouraging Initiative
So, we have had a look at some of the things that affect staff engagement, what about things that affect how much initiative people bring to their work? As I mentioned earlier many organisations still work to the outdated approach that 'senior people do the thinking and workers do what they are told'. An example of this type of thinking is detailed in the story, 'Initiative – How not to do it!' over the page.

An Outbreak of Common Sense

Pipe fitters to businessmen

So, the job of a pipe fitter is to fit pipes; all that numbers stuff you just leave to the finance department. That's right isn't it? So thought the workforce in an oil and gas fabrication business, employing 400 people, before we started to help them develop a wider view of their business.

During a two-day workshop, key staff from the shop floor were introduced to the key business principles of profit and cash and helped to see that every decision they were making every day, was in some way affecting these key numbers.

Up to that point success for them had been defined as getting a job done right and on time. It was within these boundaries that they used their initiative. With this new understanding of business fundamentals, they immediately started to apply their initiative, not only to getting the job done right, but also in a way that maximised profit and minimised the cash tied up in the process. For example, they now saw a completed pipe spool in their yard not as someone else's problem but as a lump of cash that was taking up valuable space. This was now invoiced for immediately and charged for storage until collected.

As they engaged their whole workforce in improving business performance the company saw immediate improvements in both their profit margin and their cash position. The workforce didn't change roles they just broadened their focus as to how they should use their initiative to improve things.

Let's start off by setting some parameters within which we may be looking for people to use their initiative at work.

We are looking for everyone to use their initiative <u>within</u> the context of their role or their area of responsibility.

The person who has the best knowledge of a job is the person who does that job day in and day out. They see things that others don't see. If you are going to maximise the effectiveness of your organisation, then you need to look for continuous improvement in all areas. The best placed person to come up with those ideas is the person doing the job.

Encouraging people to use their initiative at work <u>does not mean</u> throwing the rule book and the company structure out of the window!

Probably one of the most unhelpful phrases of the past 20 years has been 'thinking outside of the box'. There will always be a 'box' i.e. there are always constraints and limits in which we must work. There always needs to be a box. For people to fully commit to using their initiative they need to know the boundaries in which they can exercise their discretion. A lack of boundaries is disconcerting to people and discourages them from using their initiative. We don't need people to work outside of the box but we do need to give them a bigger box to work in!

Some of the boundaries that are required are; role and goals, legal frameworks e.g. HSE, HR etc., an individual's capability and the culture and values of the organisation. The story over the page, 'From pipe fitters to partners', illustrates what can be achieved by expanding the parameters in which you encourage people to use their initiative.

People need to <u>understand the context</u> they are working within
If people are to effectively bring their initiative to their work, they. need to understand how what they are doing fits within the bigger picture. This includes understanding what their team/department is seeking to achieve, the priorities of the organisation and future plans.

In some ways getting people to use their initiative more boils down to one simple thing; ask more questions! If you think that people in your team rarely use their initiative the first place you should look is at yourself. It's probably down to you. Behaviour breeds behaviour. If they are not using their initiative, it's because you aren't encouraging them to.

The Initiative Checklist	
Initiative area	**Score/10**
Space to act I have the right amount of space to decide what I do and how best to do it to achieve agreed outcomes	
Power I have the right amount of authority/power to make the decisions that are required to do my work effectively	
Encouragement I am encouraged by my manager to use my initiative and to challenge existing approaches to seek improvement	
Confidence I feel confident in myself to use my initiative and I have the confidence of my manager	
Involvement I feel part of an organisation where what we do matters and where I have a critical role to play	
Safe Environment We have a low blame work culture where initiative can be used without fear of unreasonable comeback and ridicule	

If you want your people to bring more of their thinking to their work, stop telling them what to do. In management terms, we might describe this as moving from directive styles of management to facilitative styles. If you are either directly or indirectly telling people what to do through your actions, then they won't think for themselves. If you lead using questions, then your people must use their thinking to respond.

Clearly there will be times when a directive approach is most appropriate e.g. an emergency, areas involving regulation or in giving basic instruction to someone new to a role. However directive approaches limit initiative and used over extended periods also have a negative impact on engagement. As such they should be used sparingly.

The Initiative Checklist
As with engagement, if you want to explore how you can encourage more thinking/initiative within your organisation, there are six key areas that can be explored easily with your team and that you as a manager can influence to a high degree. These are detailed in the checklist over the page.

PAW
The mnemonic PAW can be a useful reminder as to the three things that need to be in place for people to use more of their initiative; Permission, Ability and Will.

People need to believe that they have the permission or encouragement for them to use their initiative. This is reflected in the first three areas of the checklist; Space to act, Power and Encouragement.

People need to have the ability to be successful in areas where they are exercising their initiative. It is common sense that you should never use your initiative in areas where you are not competent! Accurately assessing ability can be a tricky though. Over 80% of people when asked consider themselves to be a better than average driver; they can't all be right! Assessing ability therefore requires both self-assessment and an assessment by the manager. This is reflected in the Confidence area on the checklist.

People must also have the will or desire to use their initiative. This is reflected in the final two areas of the checklist; Involvement and Safe environment. The more purposeful someone considers their work to be, the more inclined they will be to use their initiative. Using your initiative also involves taking a risk, you might not always get it right. You must therefore feel the environment you work in is safe enough to take this risk.

Ideas for action
Review of engagement and initiative
Using the two questionnaires from this chapter, carry out a review of levels of engagement and initiative within your team/department. You may want to add a section for people's comments at the bottom of each questionnaire. Reflect on the results: -
- What are the key messages from your survey?
- What is the one area for improvement that would have the biggest impact?
- What is your next step?

Consider repeating the survey every 3-6 months.

Motivation team session
Run a 30-minute session in your next team meeting exploring motivation.
1. Give a 5-minute presentation introducing the Four Levels of Motivation model to the team. Key messages: -
   - Each level builds on the next
   - The more positive people feel about each level the more motivated they will feel in their work
2. Check understanding with your team
3. Get each member of the team to rate their perception of each level on a scale of 1-10
4. Collate team scores on a flipchart
5. Identify the area, that you can influence, that would have the biggest impact in improving motivation
6. Agree the next steps for making this change

Personal Challenge - Partner model reflection
Using the Partner model, place where you see the various members of your team. Consider what it is that you are doing that is creating the spread of different follower types in your team.
- What could you do differently to engage different members of staff more?
- What could you do differently to encourage different members of your team to take more initiative?

Summary of Creating Partners

- Effective organisations have staff who are engaged <u>and</u> bring their initiative to their work
- Engagement and initiative are intertwined. The more engaged people are the more likely they will use their initiative. The more they use their initiative the more engaged they will be.
- Three useful questions for checking engagement are: -
    1. How are you feeling (rating out of 10)?
    2. Why are you feeling like that?
    3. What could you do that would move you one or two points up the scale?
- It is important to help people to help themselves
- Six common factors affecting engagement are: -
    1. Purpose
    2. Clarity
    3. Stretch
    4. Appreciation
    5. Inclusion
    6. Fairness
- We are looking for people to use their thinking within the context of their role
- The person doing the job is the 'expert' in doing that job
- Initiative has to be applied within boundaries or a framework
- Six common factors affecting initiative are: -
    1. Space to act
    2. Power
    3. Encouragement
    4. Confidence
    5. Involvement
    6. Safe environment
- How you lead people will be reflected in how people follow. Do you have resource, protestor, conformist or partner type followers?

Chapter 5
Contracting

If you want great work relationships, you need to pay attention to both the task and the relationship

'When I said I wanted more support from you, this was not what I meant.'

A colleague of mine was once running a leadership development course with an international group of delegates. One particular exercise on the course involved working out how to cross an imaginary shark infested river, marked out by two pieces of rope on the ground. For this exercise the team were being led by a Russian who had previously had a military background.

The exercise started and the leader stood in silence with his hand on his chin seemingly considering all the options. The time ticked on. The exercise was supposed to be completed within 20 minutes and the team became increasingly restless. Nothing they did seemed to deflect the leader from his silent reflective vigil. The team turned to my colleague and tried

An Outbreak of Common Sense

<u>Compliant</u>

'I follow because I have to'

<u>Committed</u>

'I follow because I want to'

to get him to intervene and make the leader engage with them. My colleague however did nothing, fascinated to see how this might play out. At 17 minutes the leader sprung into life,

'You will lie down across the river!' he commanded whilst pointing at one of his team members. 'The rest of us will then walk over you and cross the river.'

'But that would mean that I would die!' complained the hapless team member nominated for bridge duty.

'Yes, but the rest of the team will have got across safely and we will only be one person down,' replied the leader.

An interesting insight, maybe, into how the Russian Army used to approach problem solving! Whilst extreme, this story does highlight the consequences of leaders looking at their people as resources to fulfil their aims. I am sure that it would be unlikely that his team would be committed to his leadership in subsequent exercises!

The only person who really decides whether you are a good leader is the person whom you are seeking to lead. I have worked with many leaders who sadly seem to work to the maxim, 'I'm a great leader, it's just my people haven't recognised it yet!' I'm afraid that they are working in cloud cuckoo land.

The relationship between a leader and a team member is founded, like all relationships, on trust. The greater the trust and mutual respect between leader and team member, the more effective the relationship is likely to be.

Compliant or committed

There are broadly two ways someone might engage with you as their leader; they can be compliant or they can be committed. The lower the respect the team member has for you as an individual, the more likely they will engage with you in a compliant way. A compliant follower respects your organisational position but not you. They follow because they have to, probably grudgingly, only doing the minimum of what is asked from them. Discretionary effort or going the extra mile goes out of the window. Clearly this is not a recipe for success.

A committed follower respects both you and your position. This respect for you as their leader has probably arisen from you demonstrating respect for them. It is common sense that when someone respects both the person and their position they will do more for that person. They will do things for that leader because they want to.

An Outbreak of Common Sense

Top down
Authority
Meeting the needs
of the task

Bottom up
Service
Meeting the needs
of the team

'Servant' Leadership

The 'servant' leader

Effective leadership requires balancing the needs of the task, the team and the individual. Within an organisation, a leader will have positional authority over the team and will need to work 'top down' to ensure the needs of the task are met. If, however 'top down' is the only place the leader works from, the best they will get from their team is compliance. An effective leader will also work from the 'bottom up', seeking to meet the needs of the team and the individual.

This idea of simultaneously working to meet the needs of the task and the team might be called 'servant' leadership. In this the leader is in a position of authority over the team but is also willing to serve the team to meet their needs. The most graphic example of this is seen in Christianity when Jesus washes his disciples' feet. In WWII Field Marshal Montgomery also demonstrated characteristics of servant leadership. People under his command talked of the genuine care he demonstrated for each one of them and their welfare. Whilst Montgomery was clearly going to have to give orders that would inevitably lead to some of his men being hurt or killed, it was always felt that this was not done lightly and that he cared greatly about any loss or injury. Such leadership produces undying commitment from its followers.

If I asked you what you wanted from your ideal leader chances are your list would include things like clarity, direction, support, encouragement, challenge, affirmation, praise, feedback, honesty, openness, trust, fairness etc. It's not rocket science. These things are universally recognised as what people look for from great leaders. Now imagine if someone did all those things for you i.e. they gave you clarity, they gave you direction, they supported and encouraged you, they were prepared to challenge you, they took time to give you affirmation, praise and feedback, they treated you honestly, openly and fairly etc. What would you be prepared to do for a leader like that? Chances are that you would run through 'brick walls' for them.

If it is common sense that we will get much more from our staff if we lead them in a way that they want to follow us, why do so many leaders seem to treat their staff like battery hens or some kind of carbon based work units?! There is a Dilbert cartoon I love. In it Dilbert realises that people aren't the most important asset in his organisation but rank about 36th in a list of company resources. When asked, what was 35th his answer is paperclips!

The 'Right Stuff'

In the early years of commercial aviation, the flight crew for airlines were predominately drawn from the military. Military pilots were mainly used to flying on their own. This led to a dangerous psychological dynamic which became apparent in early crash investigations.

It was found that during crisis situations the Captain of the airline took control of the plane and became almost deaf to suggestions and input from the other flight crew. There was a strong military aviation tradition of pilots being made of the 'right stuff', heroically finding their way out of seemingly impossible situations as they battled to save an out of control plane. This left the airliner in the hands of one person trying to avoid disaster, greatly reducing the odds of success from what might be expected if all the flight crew were involved. Sadly the 'heroic' pilot was not always successful leading to many tragic incidents.

To counter this pervasive 'hero' model of leadership air crews had to go through extensive training and drills to condition them to work as a team in crisis situations. The Captain was still the leader but, through numerous drills, was reconditioned to work in partnership with their fellow crew members, drawing on all the resourcefulness of the team to fly the plane safely.

The embodiment of this new approach was seen in the 'Miracle on the Hudson'. As Captain Chesley Sullengerger sought to pilot his stricken plane to safety, after losing both engines to a bird strike, he is calmly heard asking his co-pilot, 'Got any ideas?' He went on to execute the almost unheard of feat of successfully landing his plane on the Hudson river with no fatalities.

This cartoon highlights the truth that in many organisations people are treated just as another resource and can be used in any way managers see fit. It is a particular beef of mine that most organisations call the department that looks after their people 'Human Resources'. This to me is very impersonal and somewhat demeaning. If we treat people with respect, as individuals not numbers, they will behave respectfully. If we treat people as resources they will behave as resources, only doing what is asked of them.

In the previous chapter, we explored the idea that your leadership approach will create different types of follower and that modern-day organisations require 'partner' type followers; people who were both engaged and willing to bring their initiative to their work. The idea of a working partnership between leader and follower is still counter cultural for many organisations where more traditional command and control approaches prevail. A tragic example of this leadership mindset, drawn from the world of commercial aviation, is shown over page.

It is all too easy for us to adopt the heroic leadership mindset, especially when things become tough. When we are the leader we think that we should have all the answers and take control when things become difficult. In the complexity of our world today the chances of one leader having all the answers is extremely remote. So how might we condition ourselves to work in partnership with our team members?

Contracting

My time as a manager in the bank was revolutionised when someone showed me one simple question to ask my team. The question was, 'If I am going to get the very best from you, what do you want from me as your manager?' Up until that time I had predominately been working to my own agenda i.e. 'What I want from you is........' I had not been thinking to any great extent about my team's individual needs. At best I would be second guessing what a team member might want from me. This would often be driven by trying to think what I might want if I were in their shoes.

However, all people are different. What I might want in a situation was likely to vary greatly from what a team member might want. The chances of me getting it right were not great. I worked out that the best way to establish a great working relationship with any direct report was to establish an informal contract with them. This covered three key questions; What do we need to achieve? (Outcomes), How will we work together? (Relationships) and What do we commit to do going forward? (Next steps).

Contracting in practice

With a team member

The first person that I had a contracting discussion with was a lady called Mary. Mary was a very experienced banking professional but she had recently taken up a new role as a trainer. Prior to trying the contracting idea with her, I had sought to be a good line manager, spelling out clear objectives and offering her advice as to the things that I thought would help her with her transition to the new role.

Our relationship had been ok but somewhat functional. After being introduced to the contracting idea I decided to try it out with her. I let her know that I was trying out something new and that I would really value her feedback as to whether she thought it was helpful. I also talked her through how the session would work and asked her to think beforehand about what she might want from me as her manager.

The session transformed our working relationship. I could clearly understand what she wanted from me right now and how some of my well intended efforts, up until this point, had not always hit the mark. In particular, in my eagerness to help I was saying too much. She felt bombarded by information. I was able to modify my approach and there was a step change in her performance as her confidence grew. It became a regular date in our diary, once every quarter, to check in with each how things were going, to give feedback and to agree the next steps.

With my boss

Encouraged by how things had worked out with Mary I also set up a contracting session with my boss Amanda. Again, up until this point our working relationship had been ok but I also had the sense that there were frustrations for both of us in how things were going.

I set up the time very much as I had done with Mary i.e. letting Amanda know that I was trying something new and that I would welcome her feedback. This time though I started the session by asking her, what she wanted from me as her team member if I was going to help her achieve the things she wanted. This seemed both respectful and created the right space later in the meeting for me to say what I wanted from her.

Again, there were immediate benefits from the session. The contracting framework allowed us to talk, not only about the task in hand, but also about how we were working together. The areas that were causing us frustration were surfaced and talked through, with clear steps agreed as to we could move things forward. As we continued to revisit the contracting framework over the following months we developed the best working relationship that I had ever had with any manager during my time in the bank.

A typical 'contracting' session

So, given that in most organisations having a conversation around these three questions will be highly unusual, how might you make contracting work in practice?

Preparation

My first tip, if you are trying out contracting with someone for the first time, is to chat through the concept and approach beforehand. When working with a team member it is also useful to get them to prepare for the meeting by thinking about what they really want/need from you as their leader. Encourage them to be as specific as possible. General words like direction, and support are fine as headlines but they don't exactly tell you what is wanted. Examples of questions that may help in this include: -

- In what areas are you looking for direction?
- What do you want me to do to support you in your work?
- What do you find encouraging?
- How do you like to be recognised?

The contracting meeting should be as informal as possible so agree an appropriate place for the session e.g. in a relaxed setting over a coffee. It is also best to separate 'contracting' from formal performance review sessions.

Outcomes

During the contracting meeting the first step is to agree outcomes. The key question that you should look to explore here is, 'What will define success for us by the end of the year?' It is important to be as specific as possible and to have both quantitative outcomes (hard, numbers based) and qualitative outcomes (what success might look, sound and feel like). In my experience, most managers do seek to establish outcomes with their staff, however agreed goals are often vague and difficult to measure. The more subjective the judgement of successful performance is, the more frustrating the relationship between leader and team member is likely to be.

Relationship

The core question that you are looking to explore during the second stage of the contracting process is, 'What do we want from each other if we are going to get the very best from this working relationship?' In this discussion, you as the leader need to make it clear that you might not be able, or even consider it appropriate, to do everything that is asked of you. For

An Outbreak of Common Sense

The Contracting Cycle

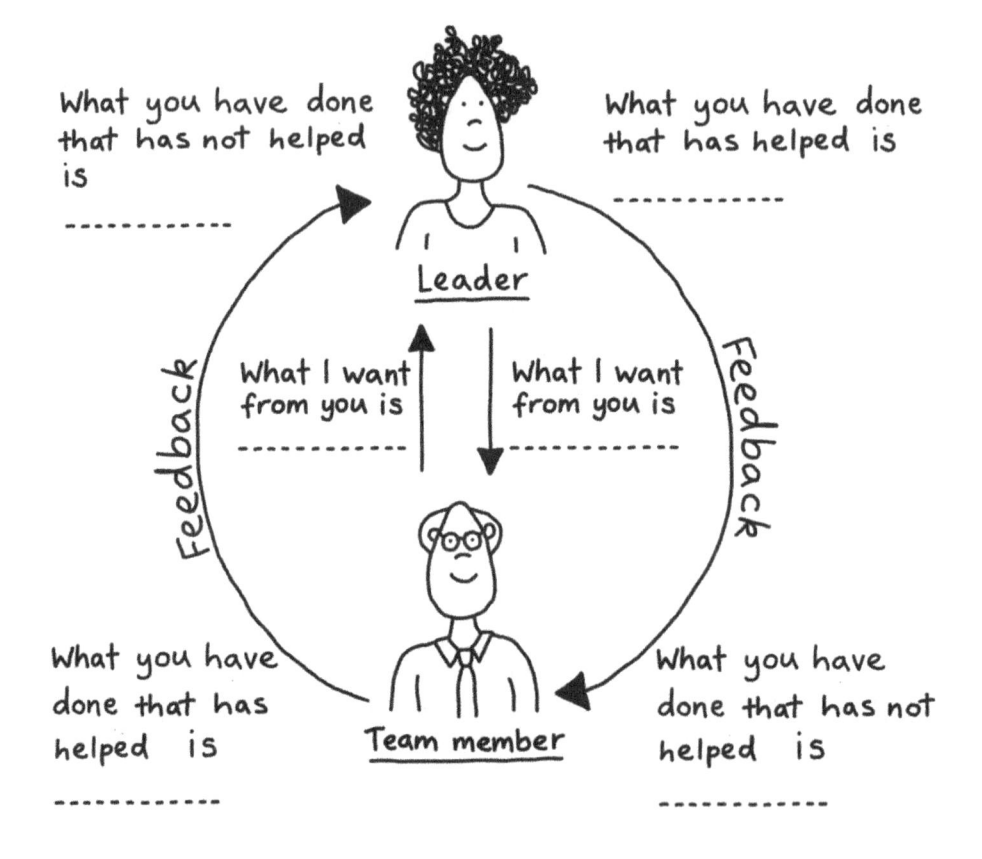

What you have done that has not helped is

What you have done that has helped is

Leader

What I want from you is

What I want from you is

Feedback

Feedback

Team member

What you have done that has helped is

What you have done that has not helped is
----

example, someone might ask you for responsibility for a particular area that you, for a variety of reasons, may not think is right. This part of the meeting will be an informal negotiation exploring what each party wants from the other. It should conclude with 2 or 3 very specific actions that you both are willing to commit to.

Next Steps
The third part of the contracting meeting is to establish clear actions and next steps. This could also include agreeing milestone performance goals. The meeting should conclude by agreeing a date to review how things are working. Contracting is an ongoing process. Relationships are dynamic and individual and organisational needs will change. As such there will always be something to explore within the contracting relationship.

Review
Within the review, you should invite feedback from your team member as to how well you have fulfilled your specific commitments and be prepared to give them specific feedback on their actions. Good feedback should contain three elements; 1) Evidence – What did someone do? 2) Impact – What impact did this have on you, others and the task? 3) Suggestions – What should they start/stop/continue to do in the future?

The review should conclude by agreeing the next things that you are going to work on to continue to develop the relationship. In essence you create an ongoing contracting cycle (see over) continually revising what you want/need from each other as the relationship develops and situations change.

Effective contracting can revolutionize organisational performance. However, even though it might appear simple and common sense, it is rarely common practice. You need to be patient and persistent if you are going to introduce this to your team. Don't be surprised if you get some very puzzled looks from people the first time you ask what they want from you as their leader. Also, when it comes to seeking their feedback about your performance as their leader, to start with you may only get very generalised platitudes such as 'fine' or 'great'. You should remember that they are busily considering whether giving their boss feedback might be a career limiting move! In my experience, if you stick with it, you will soon see the rewards both in the working relationship and performance.

Ideas for action
One Down
Run a contracting session with a member of your team.
- For your first attempt, choose a member of your team with whom you already have a good relationship.
- Prepare your thinking around the first two contracting areas; outcomes and relationships.
- Tell your team member that you are going to try out the contracting idea and explain how it works. Say that you would value their feedback as you try out the process. Give them time to prepare for the session by asking them to think about what they would want from you as their manager. Agree an appropriate time and setting for the informal contracting session.
- Agree specific actions that both of you will take.
- Follow up on these actions by setting aside time to give each other feedback.
- Persist! It is likely to feel a bit clunky to start.

One Up
Run a contracting session with your boss.
- Find an appropriate time to explain the contracting idea to your boss. Explain that you are looking to try out this idea with your team and that you would value the opportunity to also try it out with them.
- Prepare for the meeting by both thinking about the first two contracting areas; outcomes and relationships.
- Run the session and follow up as per the steps in the One Down exercise. It is probably smart to start by asking what your boss wants from you before you go on to what you want from them.
- Ask them for their thoughts and reflections on the process. You never know, you may make a convert!

Personal Challenge - Reflect on your own leadership style
- How much of a 'servant leader' are you?
- Do you meet the needs of the task <u>and</u> the needs of your people?
- How do you think people talk about you as a leader?
- How would you want them to talk about you?!

Summary of contracting
- People will either be compliant or committed in how they follow a leader
- A 'servant' leader meets the needs of the task, the team and the individual. They can simultaneously be in authority and serve the needs of their team
- 'Servant' leaders inspire total commitment from their followers
- If we are to increase our chances of success in a complex world we need to create working partnerships between leaders and followers
- A framework for contracting is: -
  1. Outcomes – What do we need to achieve?
  2. Relationship – How will we work together?
  3. Next steps – What do we agree to do over the next few weeks?
- Contracting is the foundation for creating committed followers

Chapter 6
Leadership and Management

Leaders make change happen and managers create order and stability

'But I don't understand. The plan said that you should have all bought into the change by now...'

During my time in learning and development I have become increasingly curious about the difference between leadership and management. In my experience, it seems that the higher you go up an organisation, the more likely you are to be called a leader. Being called a leader seems to be considered 'sexier' than being called a manager. Many parents would be seriously underwhelmed to be told, 'Your child is a born manager', but being told they are a 'born leader' would be a completely different kettle of fish!

Management seems to be a rather dull but worthy living; leadership on the other hand seems to symbolise transforming the world! However, when it comes to going on a training course the same material seems to be used whether you are talking about management or leadership! So is there a difference between leadership and management or is it just down to where you might be in the organisational pecking order? Is leadership more

Leadership is about creating change

Management is about creating order + stability

more worthy than management? Could you have someone who is in a senior position behaving as a manager and could you have someone behaving as a leader in a junior position? Should you be doing things differently as a leader than you would as a manager?

Working definitions of leadership and management
Huge amounts have been written over the years about leadership seeking to define and understand its nature. This material commonly explores the question of whether you can learn to be a leader or if it is just something you are born to do. Literature on the subject can be very interesting but relate little to the day to day challenges faced in organisational life. As my career has progressed I have become increasingly interested in trying to develop a practical and useful understanding of the difference between leadership and management. (The work of John Kotter has been extremely helpful to me in this search and I would recommend any of his many works on change and leadership.) These are the working definitions that I have arrived at: -

- Leadership is about creating change

- Management is about creating order and stability

These definitions are not intended to be exhaustive but pragmatic; labels and definitions that can help people in everyday organisational life to know what they should be doing and when.

When we look at the verb 'to lead' it implies various things. It implies that we must be leading something or someone. If we are leading, someone else must be following. It also implies that we are going on some form of journey. If you are my leader you must be leading me from some point to another. If you don't have anyone following you on your journey you are just going for a walk on your own! The verb 'to manage' implies some form of control or influence over things or people. In life if we say, 'I'm managing' it means that we have got things under control.

We explored in the Strategic View chapter an organisation, if it is to be successful over long periods, needs to be able to change in line with change in the world in which it works. It also needs to be able to effectively manage the challenges of daily operations. A successful organisation therefore needs to be able to change and create order and stability at the same

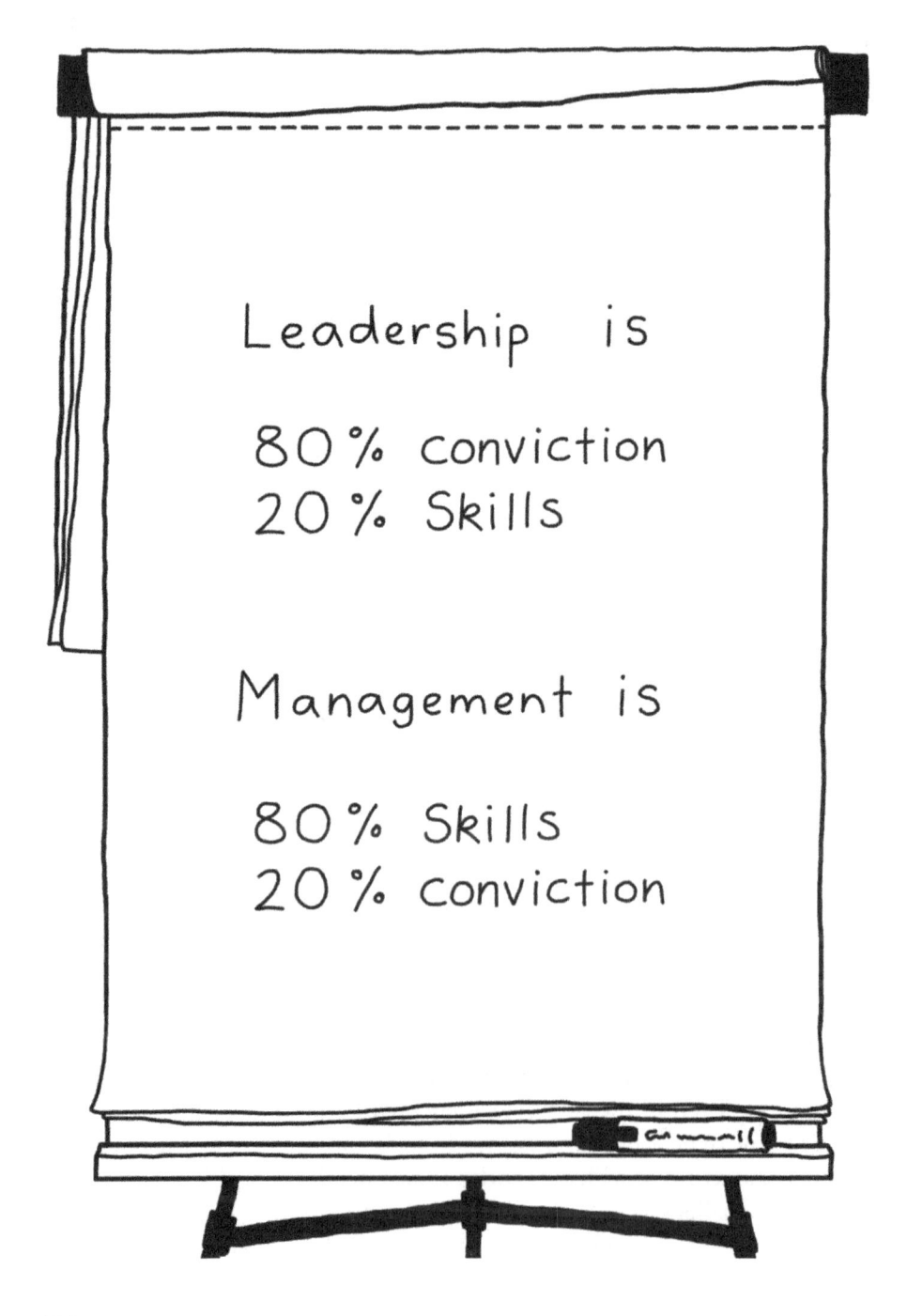

Leadership is

80% conviction
20% Skills

Management is

80% Skills
20% conviction

Leadership and Management

time. This at first sight appears mind boggling; how can you have change and stability at the same time? Well the answer lies in effective leadership and management. Both are needed if an organisation is to thrive; great leadership, to bring about change; great management, to create efficient and effective working practices. Leadership is no better than management, they are just different approaches required for different aspects of creating a successful and sustainable organisation.

So, what does this mean to you? If you need to bring about change you need to behave as a leader; if you need to create order and stability you need to behave as a manager. But what is the difference between you operating as a leader and you operating as a manager? Hopefully looking at leadership and management in the following three areas will give you some clues.

1) Conviction

The single biggest factor that differentiates leadership from management is conviction. Significant change requires effort and motivation, therefore to lead people through change you must have conviction; you must truly believe in and want the change you are trying to make happen. Throughout history those who have led change and social reform have had an overriding sense of conviction for their cause. When you ask people for examples of great leadership the most common answers are people like Nelson Mandela, Ghandi or Martin Luther King. The common factor with all these leaders is conviction; it was their 100% belief in their cause that people connected with and chose to follow.

Conviction in leaders might almost be described as a sense of calling, a sense in the leader that they believe so strongly in the change they seek, that they feel that they have no choice but to follow this path. Many leaders don't set out to be leaders but as they follow their convictions pick up followers along the way, people who are inspired by their beliefs and actions. Anybody can be a leader.

I was taken recently by the story of a lady in her 60's who became the catalyst for fundamental social change in the inner-city council estate on which she lived. The estate had become terrorised by gangs and a whole variety of anti-social behaviour. People lived in fear, often only venturing from their houses and flats during daylight hours. She became so enraged by the situation that she chose to take a stand. Slowly people started to

The Shy Leader

I spent many years supporting a leadership development programme in a large NHS Hospital Trust in London. We had people from all levels of the Trust attend the course but one of the most compelling stories of leadership came from a nurse working on the geriatric ward. At first sight she came across as quiet, unassuming and somewhat shy but when she started talking about the change she was seeking to make happen, she captivated the room.

Dementia can be a very degrading experience for both the individual and their families as the person sadly loses control of their faculties. This nurse believed with a passion in doing anything she could to maintain her patient's dignity. The area she was seeking to work in was their clothing.

Patients on the ward were compelled by laundry regulations to give up their own clothes and wear hospital gowns. Hospital gowns may be practical but they are certainly not dignified! This nurse could have just shrugged her shoulders and accepted that this was the way that things had to be. She didn't. Her passion for her patients led her to take a stand and to seek to find a better solution for them.

She went on to secure funding for washing facilities to be set up on site to service the ward. She also created systems, working in partnership with patient's families, for the patient's own clothes to be laundered within health and budgetary constraints. As she spoke, her quiet but unswerving commitment to her patients shone through. She inspired the group. At the end of her presentation she was inundated with offers of help for her ongoing work.

She had created followers.

Leadership and Management

follow her lead and the initiatives that she instigated. Over time the momentum for change built, eventually coming to the point that living conditions on the estate were transformed.

Leadership can also be on any scale, it doesn't always mean changing the world. If organisations are to be effective they require change at all levels and therefore require leaders at all levels, people who believe in the change that needs to happen in their part of the organisation and who will strive to make it happen. An example of this is shown in the story 'The shy leader' over the page.

Conviction is not a pre-requisite for management. Clearly managers need to be engaged with what they are doing and be able to engage their people but management is more of a head than a heart activity. Many of the fundamental things that you need to do as a manager can be learnt e.g. defining objectives, formulating plans, allocating roles and responsibilities, controlling resources, monitoring progress, performance management, process improvement etc. Once these core capabilities are in place a good manager can turn their hand to manage most things.

Managerial attributes are essential to establish and maintain the effective running of an organisation. They are as applicable to a senior person, who might be managing a very broad scope of work, as they are to a junior member of staff, who needs to effectively manage their own time and work.

2) Incremental versus transformational change

Both leaders and managers are involved with change. The key difference is the type of change that may be required; transformational or incremental. Every organisation should continually seek incremental improvement across every aspect of its operations. Creating a culture of continuous improvement enables the organisation to enhance its effectiveness and its efficiency i.e. it will achieve more of what it wants to achieve and will be able to achieve more for less.

Over the last 50 years approaches to continuous improvement have evolved dramatically e.g. Lean Thinking or Six Sigma. More recently these ideas, which originally developed in the manufacturing industry, have moved into all types of organisation. One dramatic example of this thinking in the world of sport was the story of the British Olympic Cycling Team. Under the leadership of Dave Brailsford, the team dramatically improved their performance by pursuing a strategy of continuous improvement he called Marginal Gains. His thinking was that if they could break down every

Management Basics

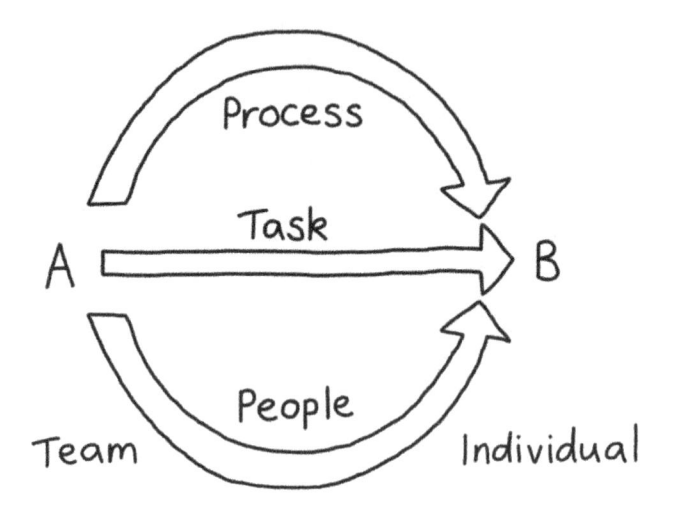

- Process
- Task: A → B
- People
- Team ... Individual

The learning Cycle

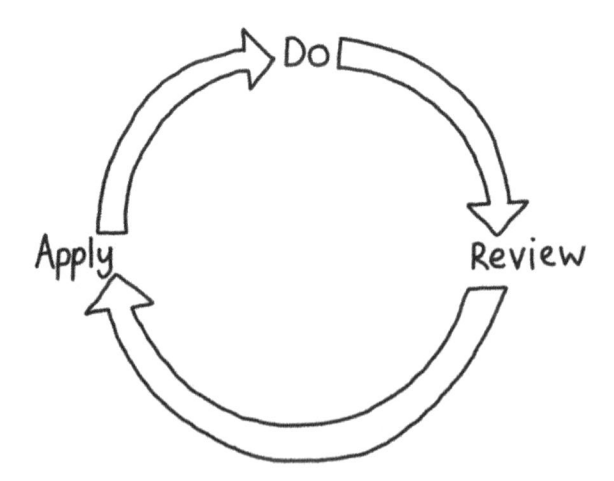

Do → Review → Apply → (Do)

part of getting an individual around a cycle track as quickly as possible and then make every bit of this 1% better, then all the small changes would add up to a significant improvement. This included every conceivable aspect of the Olympic challenge e.g. the mechanics of the bike, bike design clothing, diet of the athletes, sleeping patterns, the structure of the team, team roles, how they ran meetings, sports psychology etc. This pursuit of continuous improvement led to the team moving from winning 1 gold medal in the 2000 Olympics, to a staggering 8 gold medals in both the 2008 and 2012 Olympics.

Incremental improvement is very much a management activity. Management is about maximising the performance of every individual, every resource, every process and system and the continual refinement of approaches to do it better. One of my measures of success for any manager is that they can show that the capability of every member of their team has improved over the year. If the manager has developed capability, then performance will follow.

Effective management is about doing four things well: -
1. Establishing absolute clarity of what needs to be achieved (Task)
2. Creating excellent processes and plans to achieve the goal (Process)
3. Creating the climate for people, as teams and as individuals, to perform at their best (People)
4. Continually learning

Learning is a continuous cycle of doing something, reviewing its effectiveness (what worked/didn't work) and then applying this learning to the next plan of action. Under pressure, many ineffective managers try to short circuit this cycle and just Do, Do, Do and then try to Do even harder. Activities like reviewing, reflecting and planning get thrown out of the window as managers pursue a programme of 'headless chicken' activity. You should never confuse activity for progress. Incremental improvement requires a balance of activity and stepping back.

Creating a culture of continuous improvement also requires every member of your organisation being involved in looking for the 1% gains. For this the manager needs to develop highly engaged staff that are willing to apply their thinking to the pursuit of improvement. For more on this see the chapter on Creating Partners.

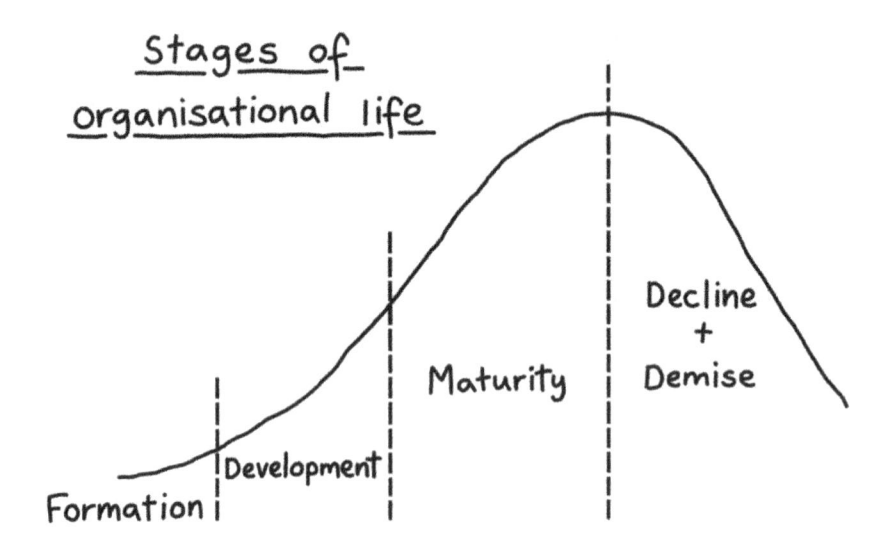

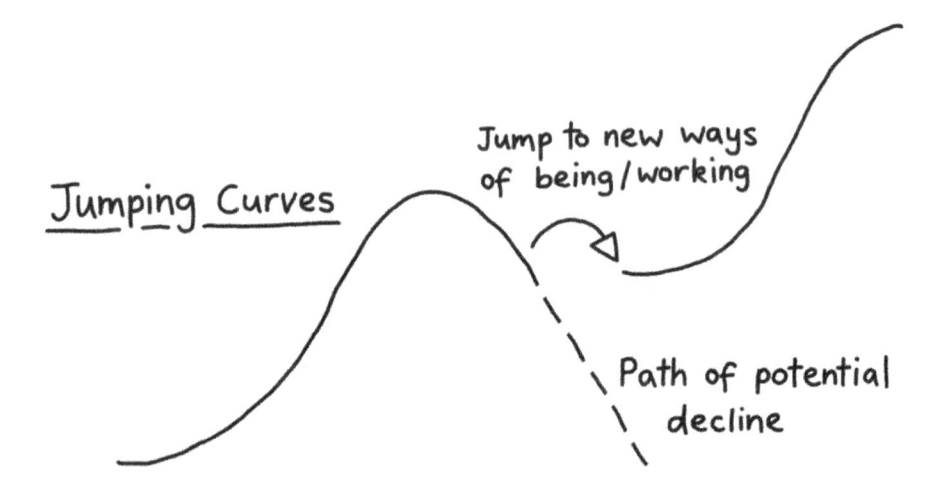

Stages of organisational life

Formation | Development | Maturity | Decline + Demise

Jumping Curves

Jump to new ways of being/working

Path of potential decline

The organisational life cycle
Whilst incremental change is part of everyday organisational life every, periodically more fundamental change will be required. Notice that I say 'will' not 'may' be needed. Every organisation over its life time will go through a number or periods of reinvention or fundamental change. This may be to respond to rapid or significant changes in the world or just be part of the normal organisational life cycle.

Every organisation has a lifecycle which can be described in similar terms to a person's life. There is a period of formation or birth when the organisation comes into existence. This can be an exciting but somewhat chaotic time as work is done without the support of defined structures, processes and systems. As time progresses the organisation settles into ways of being and doing and 'finds it feet' like the period of adolescence or young adulthood. As the organisation continues to grow and learn, it matures and refines its approach moving into adulthood. And as with humans every organisation will eventually have its day and gradually move into a period of decline and eventual demise.

This life cycle can be mapped using an 'S Curve' (see over). Each transition in an organisation's life will be marked by a fundamental or transformational change in structures, processes, thinking and approach to work. An example of this can be seen in the transition between being an entrepreneurial, dynamic and loosely structured business to a more structured, formalised set up as the business grows. This can be a very difficult time for the entrepreneur who started things off, who often feels constrained by the more formalised 'mature' organisational set up.

Not only does each stage of life transition require transformational change but sometimes an organisation needs to 'jump' to a new curve to remain viable. This leap, jumping from one 'track' to another, is a major challenge for all concerned. The size of the challenge of organisational reinvention is so big in fact that many organisations often put it off until it is far too late. Another analogy that I could use is that you need firm ground under your feet to be able to make this leap. As the organisation drifts down the path of decline the ground becomes increasingly like quick sand, eventually giving you no base to push off from, sucking you into inevitable decline.

Transformational change does not start with management. The phrase 'change management' is commonly used in organisational life. I believe that it is a contradiction in terms as management points to stability not

An Outbreak of Common Sense

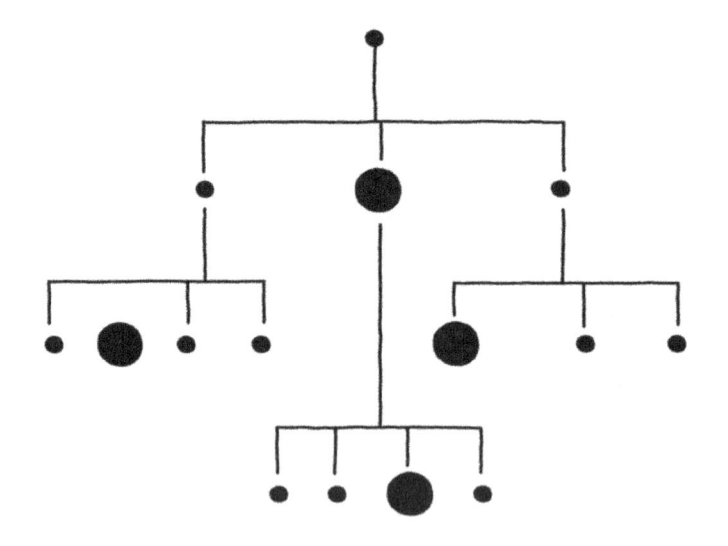

1) Formal organisation

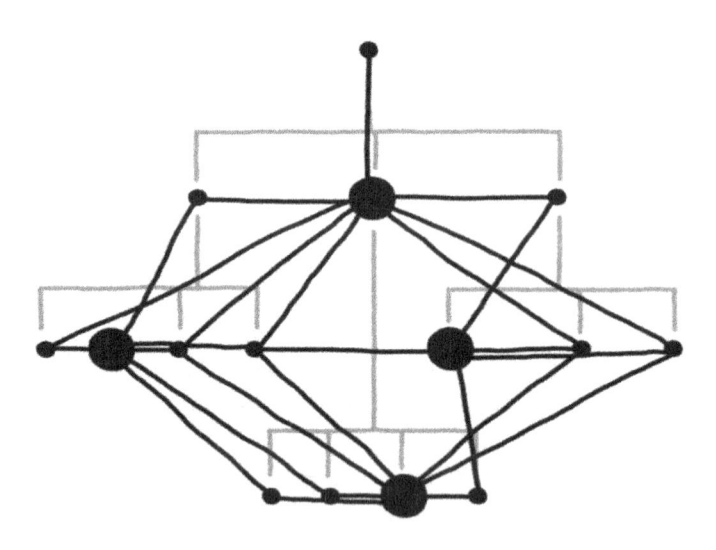

2) Informal organisation

change. People like to work to the logic that major change can be organised i.e. if we have a good plan that tells people what they should do and how they should behave then everything will fall into place. However, whilst this thinking seems sound it is fundamentally flawed. People are not always super rational, doing what logic might dictate but behave in other ways. People don't like having change imposed on them and often fear where they might end up and despite pervasive logic, dig their heels in and resist change.

Transformational change starts with leadership. Overcoming the inherent resistance to change requires passionate leaders who can inspire and positively influence people to persist and stay with the change required until completion. Sadly, what you more often see in the absence of effective leadership will be change initiatives cascading down an organisation through a series of ever shortening briefings. What might have been a three-day session for senior staff within the organisation to wrestle with the change required, becomes a three-hour briefing by the time the middle or junior levels are involved. Senior people seek to force change through by using positional authority to make things happen, wielding the 'JFDI' stick. (That's 'just flipping do it' in polite circles!) Any resistance to change is seen as a negative thing and statements like 'we need to demonstrate a can do attitude' abound. It is no wonder with this thinking and approach that few people become emotionally engaged with the change and it fails to happen.

It is not the lack of a good plan that stops major change happening, it is the lack of effective leadership! Transformation is initiated by leadership and followed up by management. Leadership creates the vision and momentum for change and then management is required to implement the initiatives and projects that this creates.

3) Viral versus Top Down

Another distinction between leadership and management is how change is delivered. Leadership can often happen outside of the formal hierarchy of an organisation. People choose who they take their lead from and this is not always from those that have positional authority. If you think of your own organisation you can probably quickly identify those people that seem to have more influence than others; those people whose opinion and behaviour others look to in guiding their own actions. This web of connections and influence makes up an informal organisation that operates underneath the formal one (see over).

Transformational change within an organisation or culture rarely

The management + leadership split within an organisation

Management

- Operational, tactical, technical
- Short term project horizon
- Deliver a great job on schedule
- Create stability + efficiency

Organisational Head
Senior Manager
Line Manager
Practitioner

Leadership

- Big picture strategical
- Medium to long term time horizon
- Health and direction of the organisation
- Identify the need for change
- Lead change

follows a neat route from the top down. Change often starts from within or on the margins of the organisation and then seems to spread through it like a virus. It is almost like change is 'caught' rather than implemented. Just look at what happened during the Arab Spring or in the fall of the USSR where the momentum for change slowly built up amongst ordinary people, before reaching a tipping point, where the sheer weight of people supporting the cause brought about transformational change.

Leaders understand and work with this viral nature of change. In seeking to bring about change they identify those people who hold the most influence within the organisation; those people who if they managed to engage with the change, would bring with them a significant number of others. The maths of viral change is impressive. If you could influence 1 person who could then positively influence 5-10 others and they then in turn each influenced another 3-5 people, you can see how the momentum for viral change can quickly build.

Management on the other hand is more of a top down process, working within the organisation's hierarchical framework. An important part of establishing order and stability within any organisation is to put in place a clear hierarchical structure with defined roles and responsibilities and areas of accountability. The authority to manage a project or a given area of the organisation comes from the position held within this formal organisational structure. As we have seen this more formalised, constrained approach to change works well in bringing about incremental change. The manager seeks to bring about change within relatively tightly defined parameters.

So what
I have offered up working definitions for leadership and management and explored how we might need to work and think differently in these two areas. But what does this mean for you in practice? Should you be a leader or should you be a manager or should you be a bit of both?

Well the answer to this is that it depends on the situation; are you seeking to bring about change or are you seeking to maintain or enhance the status quo? In reality, no matter what position you hold, you will need to do both (see over). The trick is adopting the right mindset, behaviours and approach to the issue in hand. Acting as a manager won't enable you to bring about significant change and acting as a leader won't enable you to bring about order and efficiencies.

The overmanaged organisation

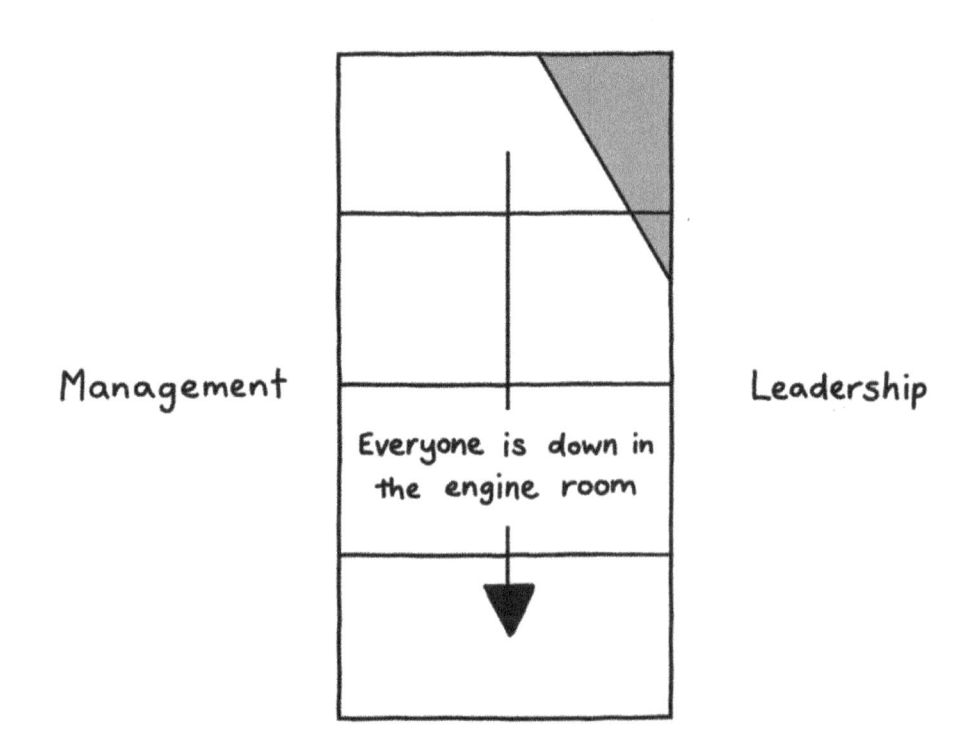

Management

Leadership

Everyone is down in the engine room

As a broad rule of thumb the more senior you become in an organisation the more you might expect the balance to shift from management to leadership. An analogy that could be used is running a ship. As you take on more senior positions within an organisation you need to shift from the operational day to day demands of running the engine room and move up to the bridge to take the big picture view of where the ship is sailing.

A practitioner or a junior member of staff may need to spend most their time just managing themselves, ensuring that they deliver what is asked of them. A CEO or MD should have very little involvement in the day to day operations but should be looking towards the long term, seeking to identify potential issues that need to be navigated and looking at the overall health of the organisation Getting the balance right between management and leadership is essential for the long-term future of the organisation. It is very easy for an organisation to fall into the trap of being over managed. When this happens, everyone gets sucked into the short term, day to day operational agenda of the organisation (see over). Everyone is in the engine room and no one is on the bridge of the ship!! There are many reasons that the management agenda can dominate an organisation. These include: -

- The operational agenda is more tangible than the more ambiguous nature of strategic work
- Operational stuff demands our attention. We believe that strategic work can be put off to another day
- We have learned how to be good managers but have rarely had the opportunity to develop into effective leaders
- Organisations over the past 40 years have got by using management approach. Senior people assume this will work in the future
- We enjoy the buzz of the everyday work – getting things done

An over-managed business steers a very risky course. Would you feel comfortable being on a ship with no one on the bridge?! The short term, operational focus that dominates the agenda leads the organisation to lurch from one crisis to the next. It never seems to get ahead of the game. Eventually the lack of leadership will lead to organisational failure.

Hopefully this chapter has given you a useful insight as to the difference between leadership and management. The following chapters will look in more detail at how you can be more effective in each of these different roles.

Ideas for Action
Management vs Leadership Focus
Take 5 pieces of paper and label and arrange them as below.
(This reflects what is central to your focus and what is on the edges.)

Almost never	Sometimes	Very often	Sometimes	Almost never

Write each of the management and leadership phrases below on to a post it and place this on the sheet of paper that corresponds with how frequently you do this. Use a different colour post it for management and leadership.

Management

Task completion, process review, tracking performance, the next month, the next 1-3 months, 12 month goals, fixing problems, operational issues, important and urgent tasks, establishing short term goals, creating short term project plans, monitoring and controls, process improvement, managing staff performance, dealing with underperforming staff, project meetings, managing budgets, client meetings

Leadership

Reviewing market trends, checking in with all stakeholders, the next 1-3 years, the next 5 years, challenging assumptions, reviewing alignment to core values, creating a compelling vision, communicating vision, prioritising critical change initiatives, listening to staff, addressing the 'health' of the organisation, coaching people through change, catching people doing the right thing, telling positive stories of change, acting as a role model for change, looking outside your organisation, important but non urgent tasks, development

As you look at the pattern of post its, what does this say about your split between management and leadership behaviours? What are the potential implications of your present focus? What might you need to do less of/more of?

Personal Challenge – Leading yourself
- What are you pretending not to know?
- What is the one thing that you believe should change but presently you are doing nothing about?
- What would have to happen for you to start to do something about this?

Summary of Leadership and Management
- A practical definition for the difference between leadership and management is: -
    - Leadership is about creating change
    - Management is about creating order and stability
- Both leadership and management are required in an effective organisation
- Leadership is required at all levels of an organisation
- Management is not confined to junior and middle ranking roles within an organisation. A person can still be in a senior position and need to operate as a manager
- If people aren't following you, you are not a leader
- People will choose who they take their lead from
- Conviction and an unswerving commitment to the change desired is one of the key differentiators between leadership and management behaviours. If you don't believe in the change you will be ineffective as a leader
- Smart leaders understand the viral nature of transformational change and seek to identify and work with key influencers within an organisation
- The management agenda and approach often dominates in an organisation.
- Change is not managed, it is led.
- It is not the lack of a good plan that stops change happening, it is the lack of effective leadership
- You will need to behave as a manager and a leader.

Chapter 7
Leading people through change

Change is both a logical and an emotional process; people don't always do what logic dictates

Please form an orderly queue to be reprogrammed for the new world

A favourite cartoon of mine is one that shows Moses standing between a parted Red Sea with the Israelites reluctantly standing on the far bank. The caption shows Moses saying, 'What do you mean, it's a bit muddy?!!' This captures for me the whole story of transformational change in a nutshell. We want all the benefits of the 'promised land' but don't want to go through the pain of the change journey to get there!

I have come across so many leaders who want the 'nirvana' of a transformed organisation but who aren't even prepared to change what they are doing, let alone invest in a comprehensive programme of change with their people. I have sat in meetings with such leaders who describe the transformation they want in their organisation, something on the scale of world peace, and then for them to say, 'and if that can all be delivered through your two-day workshop, that will be great!'

> ### Ready, Aim, Fire
> (6 principles for leading transformational change)
>
> **Ready** – Get the right people in place
> 1) Find the core leader
> 2) Put the right team in place

Let's be very clear at the outset. Leading people through change is not easy. It will require concerted effort. The bigger the change, the bigger the investment will be that is required to get there. People will get upset. As a leader, you will feel beaten up by the journey at times. Along the journey, you will doubt yourself and your ability to get there. You will require multiple initiatives to make it happen. It will take longer than you hoped. But it is possible to achieve!!!

Ready, Aim, Fire!!
So now that I have done such a good job of selling the idea of being a leader to you, let me offer you six core principles for leading transformational change. These can be broken down into three key stages: -

- Ready – Get the right people in place
- Aim – Focus and prioritise your transformation efforts
- Fire – Make the change happen

Ready
1) Find the core leader

Transformation requires energy, conviction and determination. A major change effort needs a focal point leader around which the transformation can be actioned. This leader needs four things; Clarity about the change being sought, Conviction as to why it is critical, Courage to step out on the journey of transformation and Capability to engage others in the change process.

Transformational change doesn't require a project manager it needs a leader; someone who will give their all to the change effort and work tirelessly to engage others in the journey of change. As a leader, even before stepping out on the journey, you need to do some self-reflection: -

- Are you clear about exactly what you want and why?
- How passionate are you about making this change happen?
- Do you believe it can happen?
- Are you willing to pay the cost? This is going to be a bumpy ride, especially in the early stages.

When it comes to leading transformational change, anything other than total belief and conviction in what you are seeking to achieve will seriously jeopardise your chances of success.

> ## Ready, Aim, Fire
> (6 principles for leading transformational change)
>
> **Ready** - Get the right people in place
>
> 1) Find the core leader
> 2) Put the right team in place
>
> **Aim** - Focus and prioritise your transformation efforts
>
> 3) Create a compelling case for change
> 4) Prioritise your change efforts

2) Get the right team in place to lead the change with you

As I have already outlined leading change can be a challenging and bruising journey. The leadership load needs to be shared. You need a core group around you who can help you to define the case for change, communicate this through the organisation, support your people at different points on the change journey and be a source of encouragement and insight to you.

Ideally this team should be around 4-6 people. All the team need to be totally bought into the change and be prepared to act as leaders in this regard. Your team may not be the same as that which already exists to manage your organisation. Being senior within an organisation does not mean that you are sold on the case for change or prepared to take a lead. You don't want people out front pretending that they support the change. Your people will see through this and it will undermine the change effort. Clearly you would hope to get all your senior staff on board as soon as possible but they might not all initially be part of your core leadership team.

Aim
3) Create a compelling case for the need for change

There is a proverb that says, 'Tell me and I will forget. Show me and I will remember. Involve me and I will understand. Step back and I will act.' Your message needs to be clear, simple and concise and communicated in a way that engages and involves your audience. You need to cover what needs to change and why and describe what the change will look like, sound like and feel like; this is what we will see happening, this is what you will hear people saying, this is what it will feel like. The clearer you can communicate the vision for the change, the more engaged people will be.

Use pictures, stories, metaphors and tangible examples to help people to engage with the message. Charities often do this using powerful images or stories. Those who are old enough will never forget the harrowing images of the Ethiopia famine that acted as the catalyst for Live Aid and other initiatives to combat world poverty. It is hard to deny the need for change in the light of such pictures.

4) Prioritise your change efforts

'If everything is important then nothing is. It is important to focus your change initiative into one or two prioritised areas. Change requires significant effort and will need to be done alongside the day to day work of

Ready, Aim, Fire
(6 principles for leading transformational change)

Ready – Get the right people in place

1) Find the core leader
2) Put the right team in place

Aim – Focus and prioritise your transformation efforts

3) Create a compelling case for change
4) Prioritise your change efforts

Fire – Make the change happen

5) Start with a bang
6) Build the bridge as you cross it

the organisation. There is only so much time in the day and limited will power and goodwill in your people. You can't change everything as well as maintain daily operations. Think, what are the first things that you need to happen that will provide the foundation for the whole of the change initiative. What, if we could change it now, would create the biggest impact?

I sometimes liken the change and 'business as usual' dynamic to decorating a room in your house. When you decorate one room it creates huge amounts of mess and disturbance in other rooms. If you are still going to stay in the house you can only work on one room at a time, any more and the ensuing chaos would make the house unliveable. The same is true of change in your organisation. Any change initiative will cause knock on effects across the organisation. You need to prioritise your change efforts if you are to have a fighting chance of pulling them off. Whilst it might be tempting to try and do more, this will often lead to no change being implemented at all.

Fire
5) Start with a bang

It has been said that 'change either happens overnight or it takes forever'. When you are seeking to bring about transformational change, something transformational needs to happen! At the start of the journey there needs to be something that grabs everyone's attention. It needs to be a discernible marker that we have started and are committing to this journey.

There is a huge difference about talking about change and committing to change. I have seen so many organisations draft and redraft grand statements and plans about change but never committing to it. Transformation is very easy to evidence, you either see it or you don't. Sadly, the maxim, 'after all is said and done, there is a lot more said than done' is all too true for many organisations to fearful to fully commit to change.

6) Build the bridge as you cross it

Great leaders know exactly what they need to achieve but not necessarily how they might achieve this. Robert Quinn uses the phrase that leaders need to be prepared to be 'lost with confidence' i.e. you need to be prepared to put yourself out there and back yourself and your people, to make it work as up go along. Transformational change, by its very nature, means taking your organisation to places that it has never been before. Another analogy that can be used is 'building the bridge as we cross it' i.e. we

Denial

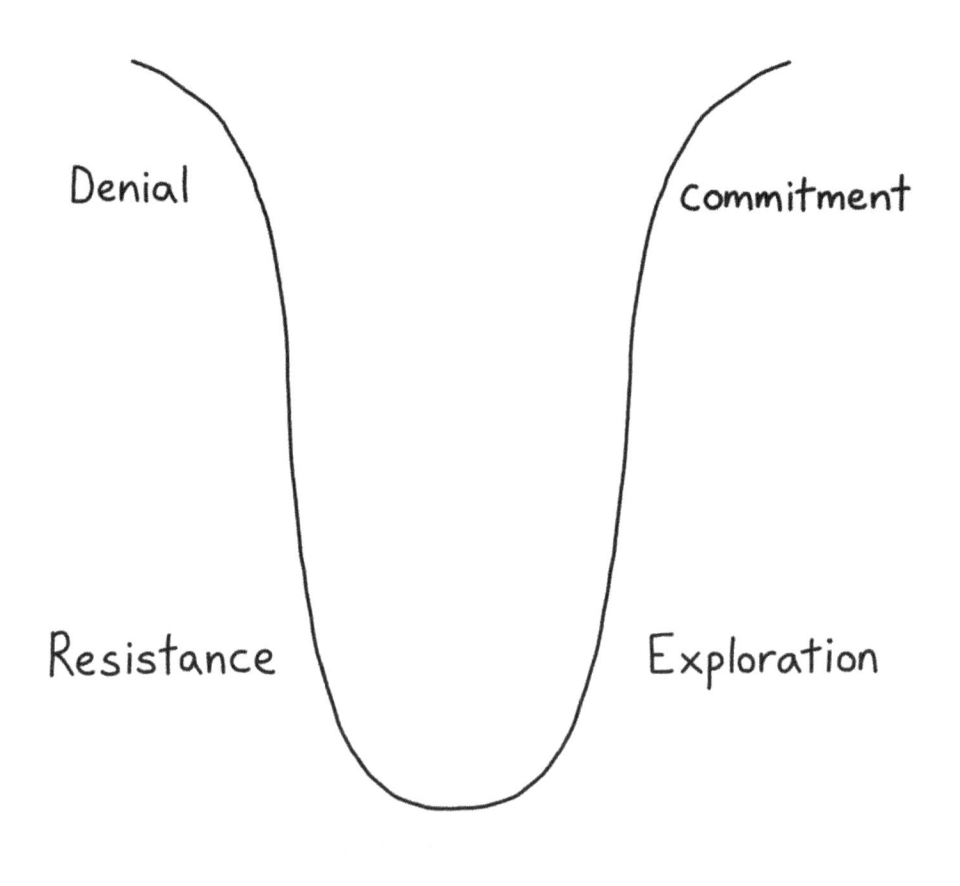

Commitment

Resistance

Exploration

The change curve

are clear about our goal but can only create the path to achieving this a few steps at a time. In this hope and confidence are essential. If these are lost the change initiative will fail.

The core source of hope and confidence is you as a leader. This is especially true in the early stages of the change journey when the end is a long way from sight. As a leader, you will need to demonstrate the beliefs that, we can work this out, we have all the resourcefulness between us to be successful and that we can work out how to get there en route.

The Change Curve

Whilst the 6 principles encapsulated in 'Ready, Aim, Fire' can provide a framework for facilitating transformational change, 'The Change Curve' can help in exploring the different tactical approaches required in engaging people with change.

Many would be leaders know that change is both an intellectual and emotional journey but struggle to come to terms with how to engage with the, less tangible, emotional aspects. They often know how to work out the case for change but then become frustrated when people don't just fall into line. Well the good news is that people might be described as predictably irrational. Whilst we don't always follow the most logical path, there are patterns in people's more 'irrational' and emotional responses on any change journey. As a leader, if you know what to expect, then you can have various strategies in place to lead people effectively through change. So let's look at some of the emotional responses to change and what you need to do in response.

Our emotional journey through change might be broken down into four areas; Denial, Resistance, Exploration and Commitment. These four areas are often shown as a change curve which tracks how a person's emotional state dips and then improves as they engage with the change.

Denial (Leader strategy - 'Confront people with the facts')
In the denial phase people simply ignore the change, pretending that it won't affect them or won't happen. Some form of denial precedes all change journeys, big or small. When Ethiopian Airlines Flight 961 was hijacked in 1996 the reaction of some of the passengers was to carry on reading their newspapers, completely ignoring the reality of what was happening around them!

An Outbreak of Common Sense

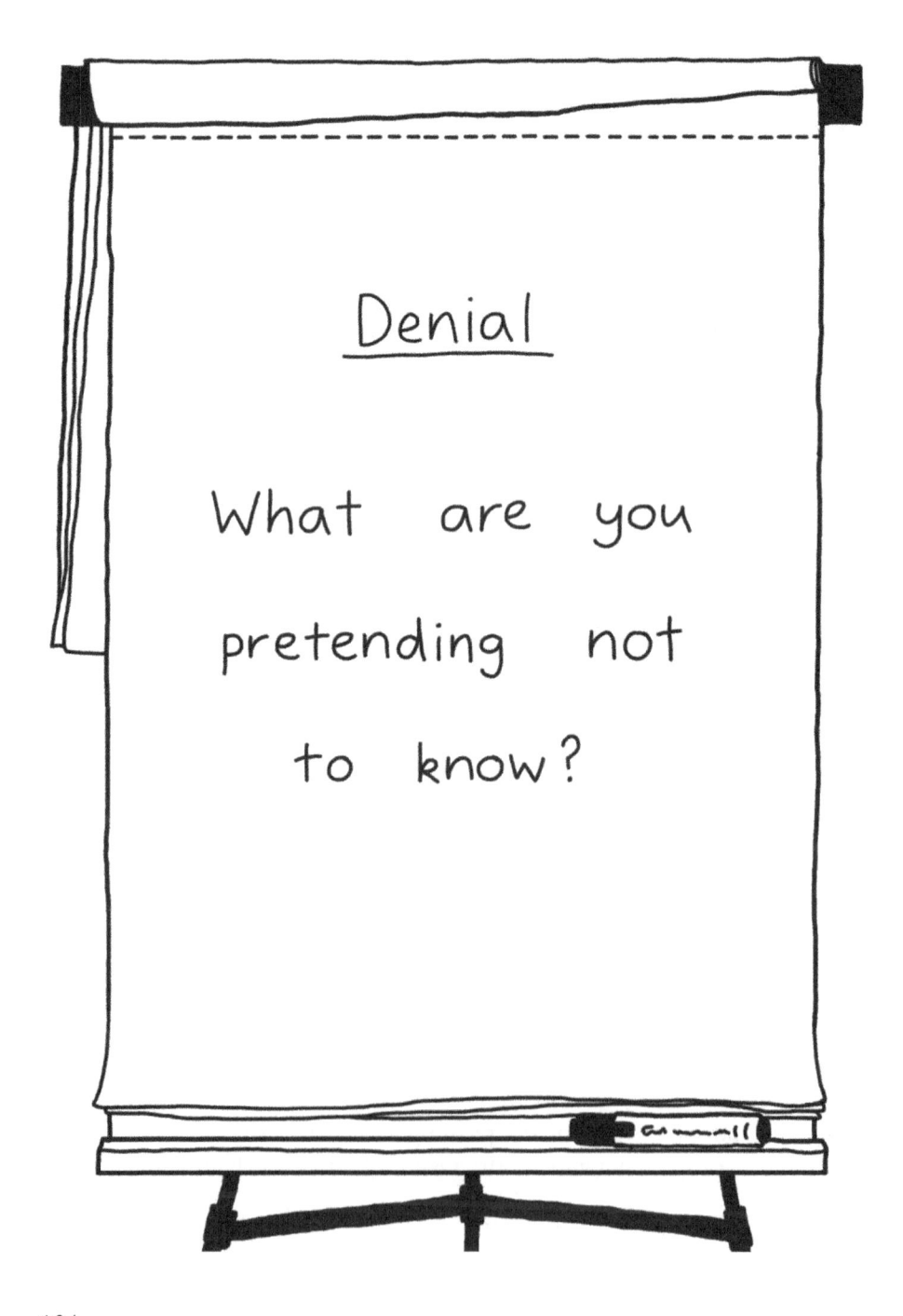

Denial

What are you pretending not to know?

As I look back on some of the major changes in my life I can also identify the periods of denial that preceded change. In 2001 I left my career in banking to move to a small leadership and development charity based in the Lake District of England. This was a huge move for both me and my family. As I look back over this time it is apparent that I had been increasingly unhappy in my banking career over many years prior to leaving. I knew in my heart that my future was not in the bank but sought to override this increasing sense of dissatisfaction by either ignoring it or by overplaying the downsides of changing things.

These examples highlight an important aspect of the emotional change journey; it is easier for others to see where you are on the journey than to see it for yourself. In the denial phase, it is the outsider that can see that things should change, even if you may refuse to hear or engage with their perspective.

As a leader, the way to deal with denial is to confront people with the brutal facts. Many organisations have failed by sleep walking off the edge of a cliff, denying the need for fundamental change until it is too late to respond. You may find the following hints and tips helpful in dealing with denial: -

- Check if you are in denial - Ask yourself, 'What am I pretending not to know?' Seek out views and perspectives from people outside of your immediate circle. Ask them if they think that you are missing or ignoring anything.
- Give people a clear understanding of why things need to change and of a positive future - Some people are motivated by moving away from bad positions; others are motivated by moving towards a more positive future. Your message needs to have a balance of both, not be all gloom and doom.
- Keep the message clear and simple and use the full range of different communication media at your disposal - If people can't see it, they won't be able to feel it.
- Expect to have to repeat the message multiple times before people get it - Many change efforts fail because the need for change is under communicated. People in denial can be very thick skinned; you have to keep 'drilling' to get through

Grumble, grumble

I remember once working with a group from the RAF in an event where they were being asked to look at new ways of working within their section. It quickly became clear at the start of the programme that the group were still pretty fed up about the change and that they weren't ready to explore how they might engage with it.

Instead of ploughing on with the scheduled agenda I decided to step back and give these guys a 'good listening to'. I asked them first to list all their frustrations and concerns on the flip chart. Then in an effort to reframe their mood I asked them to rate how frustrated they were with each point by saying the words 'grumble, grumble, grumble' louder or softer depending on how strongly they felt about the issue. We got about five points down the list before the whole room just dissolved in laughter.

Whilst the 'grumble-ometer' approach may have been somewhat quirky and unique to this event, it was built on the sound principle of allowing people to get things off their chest. The group knew that the change was inevitable but they just wanted a chance to vent their frustrations. By doing this it freed them up to engage with the change process and we went on to have a very successful programme which they all fully participated in.

Resistance (Leader strategy - 'Give people a good listening to')
As the need for change becomes apparent it often triggers negative emotional responses in people. These are primarily driven by fear e.g. fear of the unknown, fear of uncertainty, fear of losing position or status etc... This time of resistance can often seem to be the most frustrating part of the change journey for leaders. The good news to remember when facing resistance is at least your people have moved from denial!

When people are in resistance they often present their concerns through a series of, what appear to be, rational arguments as to why the change shouldn't happen. However, these presenting arguments are often a front covering more deep seated, subconscious concerns about the change. If you answer one argument, they just come back with another and so on. People in resistance do not really want to engage in an intellectual debate about the pros and cons of the change but are just saying that they don't like it.

A common phrase you may have heard people say when confronted by resistance is, 'these people need a good talking to'. In my experience the best way to deal with resistance as a leader is to do the opposite of this. What people in resistance most often need is a 'good listening to'. You need to recognise that the source of people's concerns is natural but probably more deep seated than their presenting arguments. In any change, people need a chance to 'bump their chops', blow off a little steam, have a grumble, whatever euphemism you want to choose. The story over the page illustrates one of the more unusual ways I dealt with a group resistant to change. The two things that you should not do to people in resistance are to pile on more logic or to try to stop them expressing their resistance. When confronted by resistance to change many leaders behave like an Englishman abroad. They just say the same things slower and louder! Invariably all this does is make the situation worse. Other leaders try to suppress resistance by saying that everyone must be positive about the change and treat anybody who doesn't 'toe the line' negatively.

Resistance is a natural response to any change. As a leader if you don't see it, then you should be very suspicious. If resistance isn't allowed and worked through there is a fair chance that it will become covert. Covert resistance is much more difficult to work with. People will play the game outwardly of being up for the change but privately drag their heels or even seek to undermine it. How many times have you seen people nodding and agreeing in a meeting and completely changing when they get to the corridor

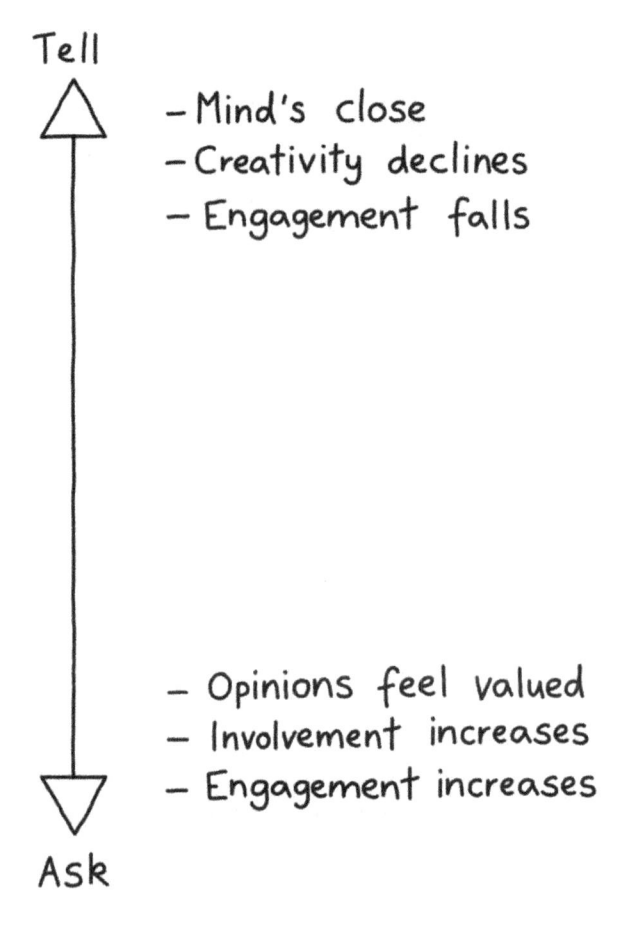

Tell
△
- Mind's close
- Creativity declines
- Engagement falls

- Opinions feel valued
- Involvement increases
- Engagement increases
▽
Ask

Leading people through change

outside? 'What a load of rubbish! I'm certainly not going to be a part of that!!' they mutter to each other as they trudge off into the distance.

Exploration (Leader strategy - 'Ask don't tell')

The next step in the change journey is exploration. During this stage people tentatively start to explore how the change might work and how they might fit into it. Some of the stronger negative emotions will have dissipated by this stage although people will remain cautious and can quickly move back into resistance if they don't like what they see.

A fundamental and common sense principle during change is the more people are involved in the change, the more engaged they will be with it. People are much more committed to implementing their own ideas than someone else's. Transformational change, by its very nature, is often difficult and complex. If it were easy, then we would have already have done it by now! It requires people to think in different ways and to do different things. It is very unlikely that any leader will have all the answers as to how to make the change happen and will need to involve everybody in solving the problem. Smart leaders are passionate about the change but not dogmatic in how it will be achieved. They see their prime role as being the focus and catalyst for change and then releasing people's innate creativity in making the change happen. It might be stating the blooming obvious but the best way to involve people is to ask them questions e.g.

- How could you make this work?
- What part do you want to play in this?
- What do we need to do to make this happen?
- What ideas do you have that will help us make this change?

It is amazing how many times I see organisations try to roll out major change programmes without effectively involving their people in the process. Tell and direction dominates the agenda as they try to regiment their people into new ways of being. It's almost like they have asked the HR department to reprogramme each person to the change by inserting a new chip into them. Even when leaders say they are 'coaching' people this often only means that they are telling people what to do in a polite way!

Recently the UK government axed a multi-billion pound project to reform the IT infrastructure of the NHS. Only months before the project was meant to go live, a survey of doctors revealed that less than 10% of believed it could work and make a positive difference. They had been working on it for up to 5 years before they asked the question!

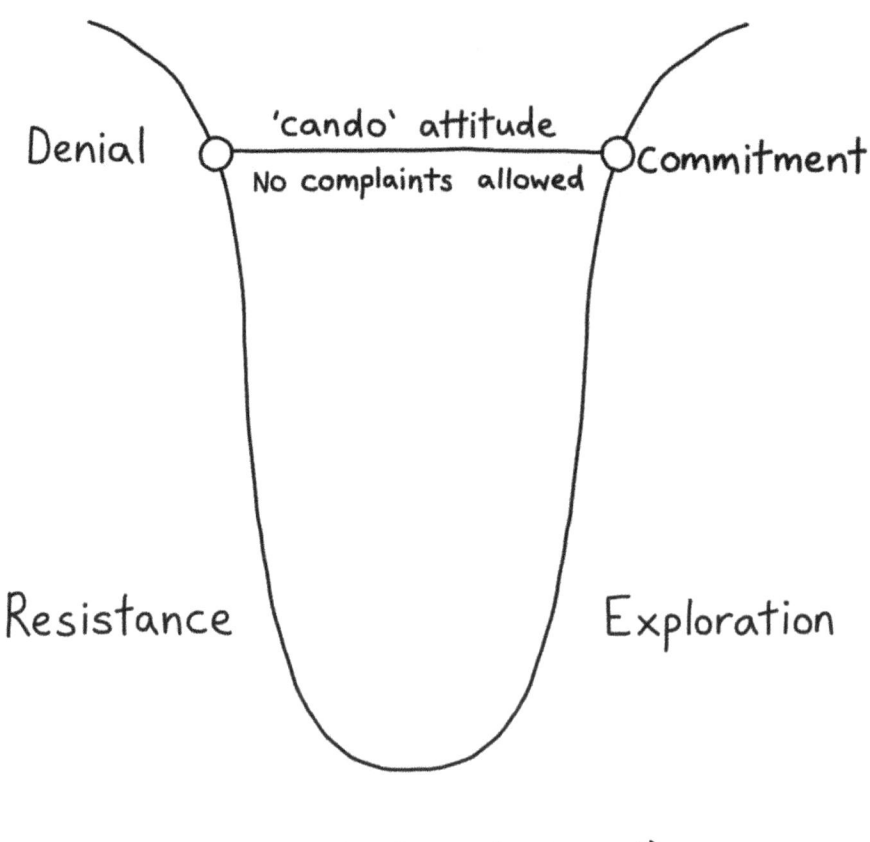

Denial ○─── 'cando' attitude ───○ Commitment
         No complaints allowed

Resistance   Exploration

<u>Trying to 'short circuit'
the change curve</u>

Commitment (Leader strategy - 'Catch people doing it right')

Commitment to change grows over time. Commitment builds as people start to implement new approaches, testing out both if they work and if they feel comfortable with them. Anybody who has tried to pick up some new skill or try something different will know that it feels a bit 'clunky' for a time. It is almost like wearing new shoes. At first, they feel a bit stiff and unyielding but over time they become worn in and comfortable to you.

We have to recognise that new structures, systems and approaches will feel uncomfortable at first and might not seem to fit with who we are. It can be very easy at this stage to give up and revert to old ways. In the early stages of any change those people who are committed to the change will be in the minority. People have a strong desire to conform and therefore at the outset, the smaller group of people up for the change, may feel pressure to stop from the larger 'no change' group. As a leader, you should spend a disproportionate amount of your time on protecting and encouraging anybody who is showing signs of engaging with the change.

A critical principle in this is 'catching people doing it right'. People learn much better with positive reinforcement. It's not just dogs that don't like having their noses rubbed in a mess when they make it! Affirm, recognise and encourage those people who act in line with the change. Make what they are doing the stories that you tell to reinforce the change. It is also a good idea to keep those who are bought into the change connected so that they can actively support each other and resist pressure from others to stop.

So, I have described here the four different stages that we need to pass through to engage with change. It sounds simple on paper but as anyone will know who has tried to initiate major change, it is much more difficult to do in practice. People don't just neatly move from one stage to the next. In reality they tend to swing forward and back on the change curve. One minute you may think someone has bought into the change, the next they seem to be throwing up all kinds of resistance again.

Leading transformation requires patience and persistence. It can be tempting to try and look for some shortcuts. This is almost like trying to short circuit the change curve whereby people can neatly make a connection from denial straight to acceptance (see over). This usually takes the form of the leader outlining the change required and then saying that they want everyone to demonstrate a 'can do' attitude, which allows no one to

Leadership Checklist

1) Clarity

   Are you clear about the change want to see? ☐

2) Conviction

   Do you have complete belief in the need for change? ☐

3) Capability

   Do you have the ability to lead people through the change? ☐

4) Courage

   Are you prepared to commit everything to the journey? ☐

question or struggle with the change. A nice idea but it doesn't work in practice. It's important to remember that people move at different speeds around the change curve and that speed can vary with different change initiatives. You need to pace your people. I have run the Great North Run on many occasions but certainly would never be described as an elite half marathon runner. Sometimes the winner of the race has already crossed the finish line before I have even started! This can often happen with large change initiatives in organisations. The leaders, who have had loads of time to think through and engage with the change, disappear off into the 'wild blue yonder' once the change 'start gun' has been fired. They completely disengage with the mass of plodders running slowly behind them, some who never even get to the start line!

Hopefully this chapter has given you a few useful hints and tips in how to lead transformational change. Are you up for it? If you have four ticks on your 'leadership checklist' you are good to go. The only way you will really learn how to be a leader is to give it a try. Are you prepared to be 'lost with confidence'?

Ideas for action
In this section I am going to make some recommendations for further reading. I have found all the books detailed below useful in developing my thinking around leading change.

The Heart of Change by John Kotter
This is one of several excellent books on leadership and change by Kotter, all of which are very helpful. In this book, Kotter breaks down leading transformational change into 8 areas. He does not propose that leading major change is just as simple as ticking off each of these 8 stages but it provides a very helpful framework for considering what needs to be addressed.

Viral Change by Leandro Herrero
All too often we look at organisations and trying to bring about major change in a very structured way. Herrero looks at things from a more 'organic' view point and explores how a major change is 'caught' as it spreads through the informal networks of an organisation. This is both thought provoking and useful, especially in seeking to identify who in your organisation might be the people that would have the biggest impact if they signed up to your change effort.

Deep Change by Robert Quinn
I found Deep Change very helpful in thinking about where I was personally in times of big change. The concept of being 'lost with confidence' has had a profound impact on both my business and personal life i.e. recognising that major change doesn't have a route map but being confident in my abilities and the abilities of people around me to work it out a step at a time.

The Chimp Paradox by Steve Peters
Understanding how people work is important if you are going to be an effective leader. Steve Peters has turned around the performance of many top sports people. In this book, he uses a simple but powerful metaphor to explain how different parts of our brain work which illuminates why people might behave and respond in the way that they do.

Summary of leading people through change
- Change requires effort and investment
- 6 principles for leading transformational change can be summarised in three stages Ready, Aim, Fire
  - Ready – Get the right people in place
  - Aim – Focus and prioritise your transformation efforts
  - Fire – Make the change happen
- Change is both an intellectual and an emotional journey
- Simple logic doesn't prevail but people might be described as 'predictably irrational' in their emotional responses to change
- The change curve highlights four different stages that we will pass through when dealing with change
  - Denial
  - Resistance
  - Exploration
  - Acceptance
- The headline strategies to lead people through each stage of the change curve are: -
  - Denial - Confront people with the facts
  - Resistance - Give people a 'good listening to'
  - Exploration - Ask don't tell
  - Acceptance - Catch people doing it right
- Leadership checklist
  - Clarity – Are you clear about the change you want to see?
  - Conviction – Are you clear on why the change needs to happen?
  - Capability – Can you lead people through the change?
  - Courage – Are you prepared to commit to the journey?

Chapter 8
Management Basics

If you treat people like numbers, they will behave like numbers

Some of the team were wondering if your management style was a bit too directive for the council's social housing department!

'For every person who's a manager and wants to know how to manage people, there are 10 people who are being managed and would like to figure out how to make it stop.'

Scott Adams

Management really isn't that sexy. One of the signs of being a great manager is that you are barely noticed at all; your team seems to run like a well-oiled machine, effortlessly and efficiently delivering results with seemingly little or no senior level interventions. If management is done badly though it can make the lives of those being managed a complete misery.

The most effective managers that I have come across regularly credit their success to being lucky enough to have a great team. It's amazing how this 'luck' remains with great managers even as personnel within their teams change. It's not luck; it's down to the skill of the manager in creating the right environment for individuals and the team to thrive.

Management Basics

```
         Process
      ⌒⌒⌒⌒⌒⌒⌒↘
A ══════ Task ══════▶ B
      ⌣⌣⌣⌣⌣⌣⌣↗
         People
Team              Individual
```

The role of effective management remains a fundamental part of the success of any organisation. Many studies have cited the fact that people don't leave organisations, they leave managers. Managers are at the front line of staff engagement and task delivery. Management basics are common sense, the challenge is effective execution.

I introduced the management basics model in the chapter on leadership and management. This breaks effective management down into three areas: -

- The task – What do we need to achieve?
- The process – How will we go about achieving the task?
- The people – How will we maximise the performance of the team and each individual?

In this chapter, we will explore what effective managers do in each of these three areas and how you need to vary your management style to achieve the best results.

Managing the Task

It really can't be overstated how important it is to be clear about the task at the start of any management challenge. The clearer you are about the 'what', the easier it becomes to do the 'how' and engage people in the process. Clarity is not just about defining the desired outcome but also the parameters within which it must be achieved. For example, in business it is not enough to produce your product or service to high standard, it needs to be done within certain cost parameters to be profitable and produced in an ethical manner.

Most organisations run to the unwritten rule that, 'what gets measured, gets done' i.e. the thing that managers pay the most attention to is what people prioritise, regardless of wider implications. For a time in the National Health Service waiting lists became the number 1 priority and a target of a maximum of 18 weeks wait was set. This didn't always lead to better patient care as quick doesn't always mean good. As pressure to hit the target increased hospitals also started playing games with their admin procedures to create the impression things were on track.

Having the right blend of goals and being totally clear about the parameters within which these must be achieved, is hugely important. There can be a tendency to over emphasise those things that are easy to measure. There are two types of goal; quantitative goals and qualitative goals. Quantitative goals are outcomes that can easily be defined by a number e.g. sales

SMART Objectives

The SMART goals mnemonic has been commonly used for many years but it probably bears recapping briefly. Each letter points to one aspect of defining a clear goal.

Specific — What exactly are we trying to achieve?

Measurable — How will we know when we have achieved it?

Achievable — Is this realistic?

Relevance — Why is it important that we achieve this?

Timed — When does this need to be achieved by?

This is all common sense stuff but it still is a very useful checklist of questions to follow in defining effective goals.

volumes, profits, days worked etc. Qualitative goals are defined by the qualities that you might want to see as an outcome e.g. Customer satisfaction, staff engagement, team working etc. You will know when you have achieved a qualitative goal through what you see, hear and feel. Whilst tricky to define in words you will know if you have achieved a qualitative goal e.g. you know very quickly if a team is happy and engaged or a customer is satisfied with your service.

Finding the right balance of quantitative and qualitative goals is essential in defining a task effectively. Sociologist, William Bruce Cameron captured this in his quote, 'Not everything that can be counted, counts. Not everything that counts can be counted.' The banks would not have lost billions of pounds in mis-sold insurance penalties if success had been defined by both a revenue target (quantitative) and an ethical customer service target (qualitative).

The desire to dive into action in most modern-day organisations means tasks are often very poorly defined. I have seen countless examples of this leading to huge amounts of wasted time, effort and resources, and huge frustration to everyone involved. Stepping back, taking the time to properly define the task and ensuring everyone fully understands this, is always a worthwhile investment. The mnemonic SMART is useful when setting goals (see over).

Managing the Process
Dwight Eisenhower said, 'In preparing for battle I have always found that plans are useless, but planning is indispensable.' Many military leaders will tell you that their plan only survives the first five minutes of any engagement.

The world has a habit of changing and undoing our most finely crafted plans and processes. With this in mind you should hold lightly to any plan to allow for flexibility in implementation. Any plan is your best guess at this stage as to the best way to proceed. As you implement the plan there will always be new discoveries and challenges that the plan needs to work around.

In formulating your process to achieve a task you also need to be careful not to fall into the trap that this is the manager's job. It is certainly the manager's role to ensure that there is a clear process in place but wherever possible, coming up with the ideas should involve the whole team. We have seen in other chapters that the more we involve people, the greater the

Process Improvement

1) Define the area for improvement
2) Analyse the area for improvement
3) Identify the root cause for any issues
4) Generate ideas
5) Implement, review + standardise

engagement we will see. People are far more committed to implementing their own ideas and will value being involved in the process. Key questions in establishing an effective process include: -

- What resources do we have at our disposal?
- What capabilities do we have within the team?
- What additional resources and capabilities might we need to secure?
- What are the constraints within which we must operate?
- Roles and responsibilities – who will do what?
- Milestones – how will we know that we are on track?

Process Improvement

In many cases as a manager you will not be devising new processes but seeking to improve existing ones. The 5-step process improvement plan (see over) is a useful guide to follow when seeking to manage incremental improvement.

Step 1 - Define the area for improvement

Process improvement doesn't always have to be about fixing problems; in fact, looking at process improvement with a problem mindset may limit progress i.e. you only act if you see an issue. The problem mindset might be described by the maxim, 'if it's not broke don't fix it!'. Continuous improvement is built on the idea of seeking to improve every part of a process, even if these parts are working ok.

A useful concept in defining the area for improvement is 'bottlenecks'. In this you are seeking to identify the weakest part of the process to work on. Process improvement in organisations often takes little account of where the bottleneck in the system is. This is potentially risky as improvements in another part of the system, away from the bottleneck, could cause increased pressure on the bottleneck. An analogy for this is passing water through a pipe. If one part of the pipe is constrained, turning up the water pressure will only increase the risk of the whole pipe failing. Water can only flow as fast as the narrowest point in the pipe allows. Well intentioned improvement efforts in the wrong area may therefore lead to an overall drop in performance.

An Outbreak of Common Sense

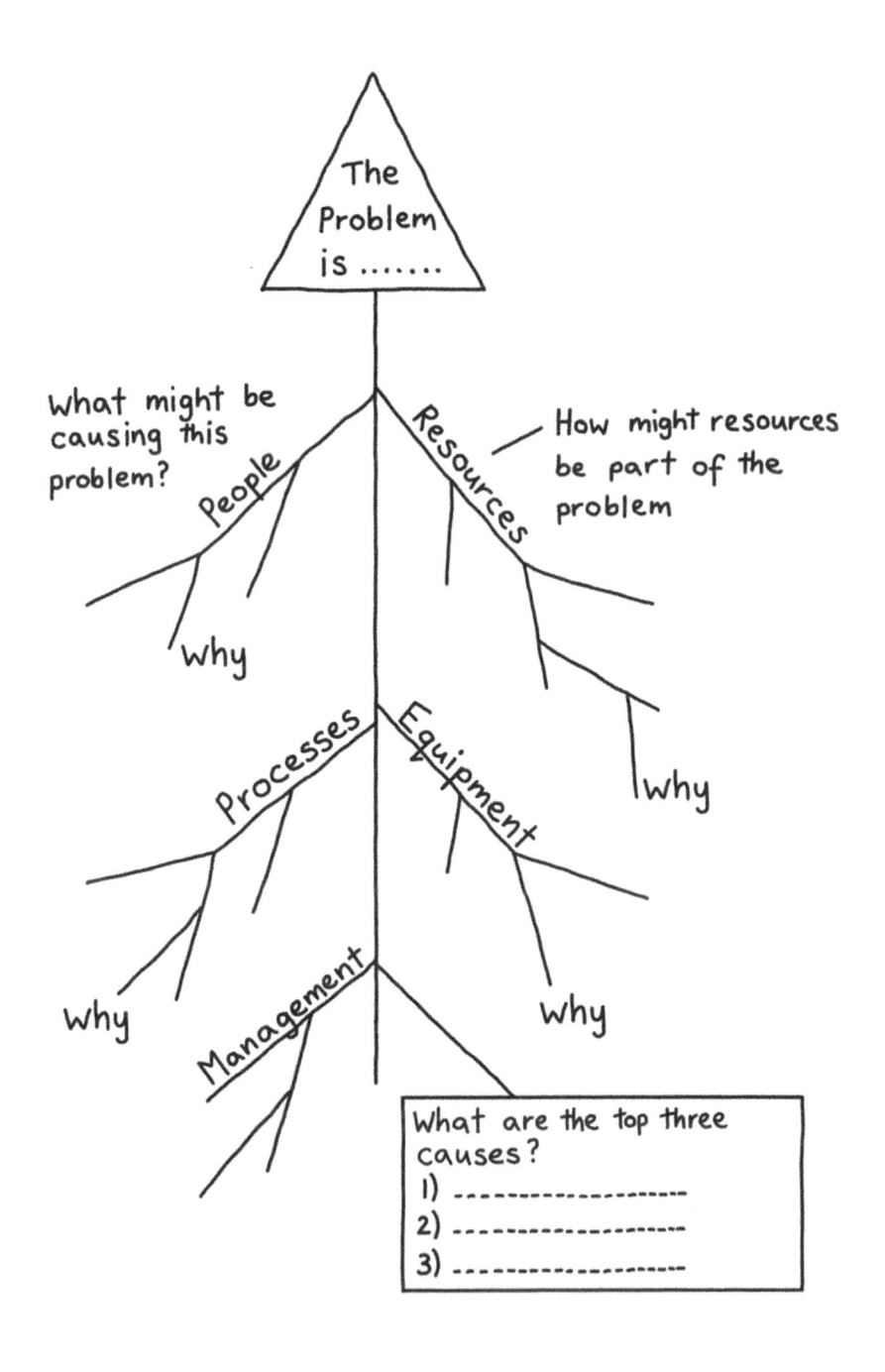

The Problem is ....

What might be causing this problem?

People

why

Resources

How might resources be part of the problem

why

Processes

Equipment

why

why

Management

What are the top three causes?
1) _____
2) _____
3) _____

Step 2 - Analyse the area for improvement

It's important to gather as much data as possible to fully understand what is happening in the area you are seeking to improve. If this is a physical process you should go and see what is happening and speak with the people involved. Effective analysis will allow you to accurately define what is happening and who is involved. The data gathered will also provide the foundation for devising key success measures for tracking improvement. For example if you found out that part of an issue was that people lacked knowledge about a certain process, you could seek to introduce a short test in the future to ensure that this was no longer the case.

Step 3 - Identify the root cause of any issues

It is easy, in busy organisational life, to fall into the trap of looking for quick fixes. This happens when exploring any issue is done superficially and quick solutions are sought. The problem with quick fixes is that they can come back to bite you as they fail to address the underlying issue. For example, you could deal with an issue of underperformance by passing parts of that person's work to other people. In the short term this may get the work done. However, this is likely to undermine the confidence of the person being 'rescued'. This and the potential risk of overloading the other people, is likely to cause more significant performance issues in the future.

Two useful tools to explore the root cause of any issue are Fishbone Analysis and the Five Whys. Fishbone analysis, (see over), places the issue at the 'head' of the fish and then maps potential causes, on the body, by exploring the question, 'What may be contributing to this problem?' Sometimes it is helpful when using this tool to frame your exploration of the issue using 4-5 generic areas e.g. people, resources, processes, equipment and management. When you have identified all the potential factors leading to the issue you can use the 80/20 rule to identify the biggest contributing factors i.e. what are the 2 or 3 issues that are contributing most to this problem. These few areas then become the place to concentrate your improvement efforts.

Fishbone analysis can be used in conjunction with the second root cause tool, The Five Whys. The Five Whys simply looks at an issue and asks the question, 'Why?' You then repeat the question, several times, going deeper each time. For example, if I had broken down on the motorway the Five Whys might look like this: -

Working with the 5 whys

- Ask why something has happened up to 5 times

- Uncover the underlying human issue

- Look for solutions to each level explored

- Chip away at improving the underlying issues

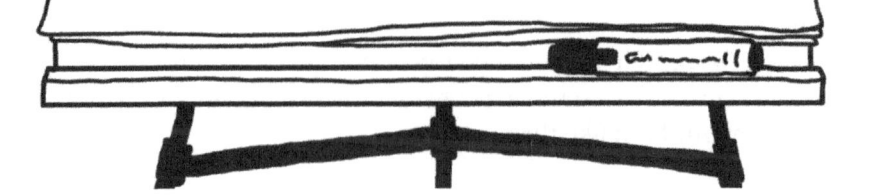

Management Basics

1 - Why did you break down?	The engine seized.
2 - Why did the engine seize?	It ran out of oil.
3 - Why did it run out of oil?	I failed to get it serviced.
4 - Why didn't you service it?	I was too busy
5 - Why were you too busy?	I am poor at time management

You can see from this example that what started out as a mechanical problem had its roots in a human problem i.e. my inability to manage my time effectively. It is useful when using the Five Whys to drill down until you find the underlying human problem that is always there. In resolving the problem, you will need to find solutions for all the levels. In my example I need a short-term fix to get my car going again but I also need a more fundamental solutions to ensure I don't miss services in the future. Failure to do these would mean that I would likely find myself stranded again at some future date! A short summary of how use 'The 5 Whys' is detailed over.

Step 4 - Generate ideas

In looking to generate ideas for process improvement you should seek to come up with as many options as possible. In the early stages of generating ideas your brain will come up with the 'usual suspects' i.e. ideas that you have thought of and possibly explored before. The real gold nuggets of performance improvement come from pushing past these ideas into the territory of 'what else could we try?' You may find this takes some effort and may lead to some uncomfortable silences as people have to stretch their thinking. Finding the right space and time to allow this process to happen is therefore very important.

Generating ideas is not about trying to find the 'golden bullet' or killer idea. You should look to generate a bank of potential ideas that you might be able to draw upon over time. Continuous improvement is an ongoing process of journeying around the learning cycle, trying an idea, reviewing its effectiveness and generating further options. In this having a range of different ideas at your disposal is invaluable.

Step 5 - Implement, review and standardise

The final stages of process improvement involves trying out new approaches, reviewing their effectiveness and then if the idea is considered worthwhile, standardising it so that it becomes part of everyday work. When standardising an idea, it is important to make it as difficult as possible to go back to old ways of working until the change is consolidated

An Outbreak of Common Sense

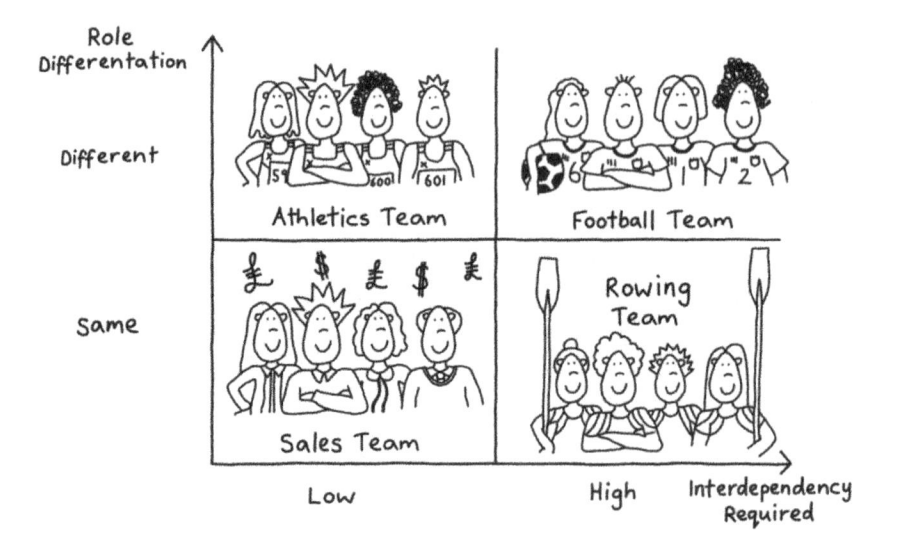

	Athletics Team	Football Team
Role Differentiation: Different	Athletics Team	Football Team
Same	Sales Team	Rowing Team
	Low	High → Interdependency Required

Managing the People

People issues are often called the 'soft stuff' of organisational life. This label is very unhelpful as it downplays the importance of effectively managing people. In fact, how well people are managed is one of the single biggest factors that will affect the performance of any organisation. There is no point having the smartest and most capable people in the world if you can't get them all pulling in the same direction. People issues are really the 'hard stuff' of organisational life.

Managers may shy away from the people issues as they struggle to understand what is going on and how they should intervene. There is often a fear that seeking to address people issues may make things worse. It is probably helpful to explore managing people effectively in two areas; 1) How to get the best from your <u>team</u> 2) How to get the best from <u>individuals</u>.

How to get the best from your team

I am frequently asked to run team-building events. The first question I ask is, 'Have you got a group or a team?' Building a team requires a lot of time, energy and resources. Not every group though needs to be a team therefore team building may be a waste of time. The key factor that differentiates a group from a team is how much individuals need to work together, or are dependent on each other, to achieve the goal. A group has a common goal but low levels of interdependency; a team has a common goal with high levels of interdependent work required. The simple model over the page might help you decide what type of group/team you might have/need. It explores two areas; how much do individual roles differ within the team and how much interdependent working is required within the team

The Sales Team Type – is more of a group than a team. The group has a common goal but this is mostly achieved by individuals working independently. Within sales groups the independent nature of the work is often reinforced by tracking performance on a league table, with individuals working in competition against each other to secure higher rewards. If you track your team's performance by using a league table don't expect them to share best practice and ideas. In a sales group this is not a problem as more is often gained in performance from the completive environment than is lost by the lack of interdependent working.

The manager's role in leading this type of group is to try to maximise individual performance. There really is little point in seeking to invest in

An Outbreak of Common Sense

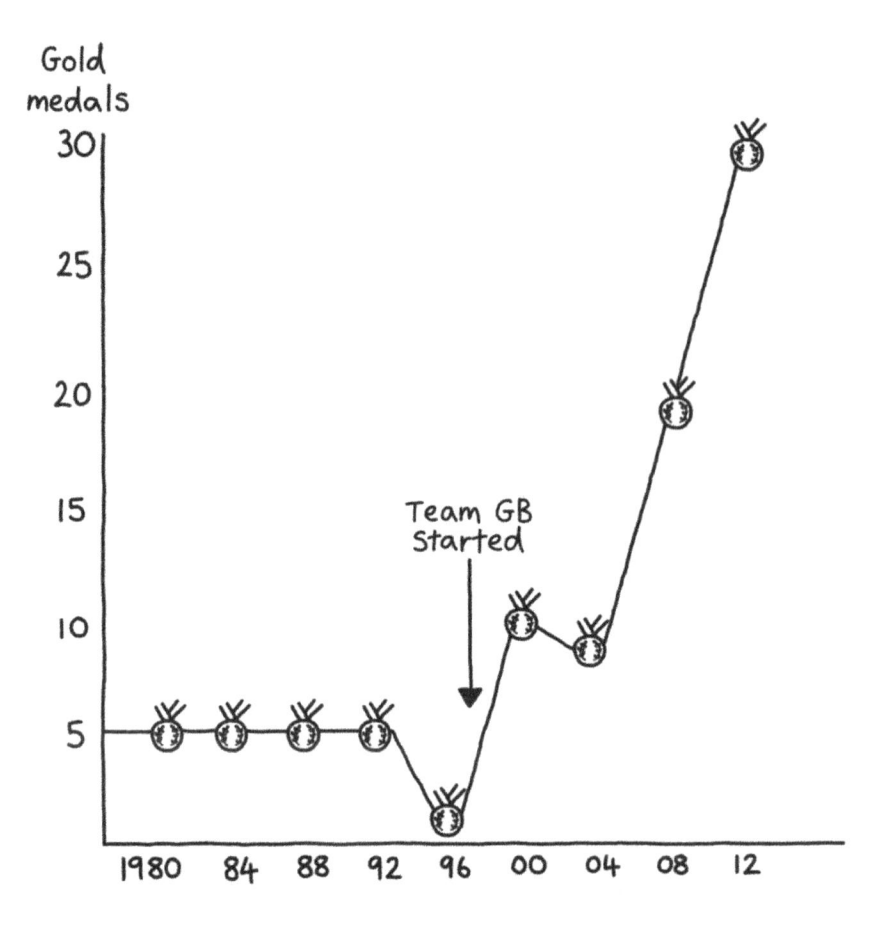

Gold medals

Tracking the performance improvement of Team GB

building a stronger team dynamic as this investment in time and effort will bring little reward.

The Athletics Team Type - has a loose common goal but delivery of this is mostly down to individual efforts. Again, the word 'team' is probably more of a misnomer as this really is a more of a group. Up until more recent times the manager of an athletic team would have made little or no investment in building the team. Athletes would have rolled up to the event, put on their team shirt and then got on with their own event.

The Team GB idea in British sport though has shown the benefits of seeking to build a stronger shared identity amongst this type of group. The Team GB idea was built on the thinking that 'together we are stronger'; our needs as individuals are better served by trying to work together to create a 'bigger pie' from which we can all benefit. By investing in the common brand of Team GB, individual sports have been able to secure increased levels of funding and at big sporting events, benefitted from the buzz that being part of a successful bigger team creates. The graph over the page shows the dramatic improvement in Olympic performance seen since the introduction of the Team GB idea.

Professional services organisations, medical and academic institutions fit this type of group working. The manager in this instance plays more of a coordinating and facilitative role, seeking to create the very best conditions for individual performance to thrive, whilst still trying to develop a sense of the group's overall presence.

The Rowing Team Type - requires high levels of interdependency and coordination. If any of the rowers is out of step with their team members, the potential clashes of oars can lead to catastrophic outcomes. With a rowing team success is built on developing high levels of team work and understanding. Teams involved in manual labour and physical tasks fit into this category of team. The manager's job here is to support the development of the common skills required and to invest in developing a strong close bond between individual members of the team. Doing this will develop a skilled and cohesive team.

The Football Team Type - is the most challenging for a manager to lead. It requires high levels of interdependency but also the coordination of different roles within the team. Success is dependent on mutual understanding

Team Purpose and Goals	1	2	3	4	5
I am clear about the purpose of my team					
My team pulls together in the same direction					
My goals are consistent with the team's goals					
I know the team's 3, 6 and 12 month goals					
I am clear how we will achieve these goals as a team					
Sub total (number of ticks X the column value)					
Section total (Total of all columns)				/25	

Team Roles	1	2	3	4	5
I clearly understand my role in the team					
I understand the roles of every team member					
I am clear where we need to work closely together					
We regularly review team roles to minimise conflict					
I understand how team members prefer to work					
Sub total (number of ticks X the column value)					
Section total (Total of all columns)				/25	

Team Processes	1	2	3	4	5
We have regular robust and effective discussions					
Our meetings are compelling; never boring					
Discussions always conclude with clear actions					
We hold each other to account					
There is clear and effective leadership of the team					
Sub total (number of ticks X the column value)					
Section total (Total of all columns)				/25	

Team Relationships	1	2	3	4	5
I am clear about our team values					
We have high trust relationships across the team					
People challenge poor behaviour					
Secrecy and hidden agendas are discouraged					
There is a positive work climate within the team					
Sub total (number of ticks X the column value)					
Section total (Total of all columns)				/25	

and team work. Another great example of this multi-disciplinary type of team is a trauma care team in an Accident & Emergency unit. The high levels of teamwork seen in teams such as these are the result of significant levels of investment by the manager in developing the team away from the demands of the task. It should not be underestimated how much work is required in creating a high performing team. Work has to be done in building relationships and developing mutual understanding between team members and in 'choreographing' how the various roles will work with each other to complete the task.

Team effectiveness framework
When people come together to work as a team there will always be some friction and waste. A graphic illustration of this is seen in a tug-of-war team. If you put 8 people together, each of whom could pull 100kg, the most they would be able to pull together would be around 600kg. Some of the individual capability would be lost in slight inefficiencies in working together and coordinating efforts.

You may have been part of a team and thought that you could do more if you were left on your own. This to some extent could be true as working with other people does create distractions. The point is that you would never achieve the whole task on your own. You therefore have to work in a team and put up with the inherent frustrations that comes with this.

A useful framework in developing your team looks at 4 areas: -
- Goals – How clear is everyone about what needs to be achieved?
- Processes – How best will we work together to deliver the task?
- Roles – Who is responsible for what?
- Relationships – How are we working together?

I have included a short review questionnaire to help you to explore some of these areas with your team (see over). The questionnaire will highlight how effective your people perceive the team to be and potential areas to work on.

As you seek to develop your team you make seek assistance of an external facilitator. This can be particularly helpful when exploring relationships within your team. The facilitator looks after the process of team development, freeing you up to participate fully in the discussions and ensures that clear actions are identified.

4 Step Performance Management

Step 1 – Establish role clarity

Step 2 – Agree minimum expectations

Step 3 – Monitor performance and review effectiveness

Step 4 – Make appropriate management interventions

How to get the most from an individual
As a manager, you not only need to pay attention to the needs of the team but also to the needs of each individual. If an individual is to remain engaged with a team and the work, there must be something in it for them. If an individual feels that they are always 'taking one for the team', their patience will wear thin.

So how might you best manage the performance of individuals in your team? It is interesting that in many organisations the term 'performance management' has become linked to underperformance. Managers seem to spend most of their time dealing with the handful of people within their teams who are not hitting the mark. This sends out the message to staff, 'if I need to work with you, there's a problem'. This is short-sighted and undermines the overall performance of your team. You should seek to improve the performance of every member of team; in fact, improving the performance of your high performers is likely to bring you the highest dividends!

This four-step performance management process (see over) has been very helpful to me when I have been in a management role

Step 1 – Establish role clarity
Being totally clear about a person's role provides the foundation for effective performance. This step seems so obvious it is often overlooked or done very poorly. A useful exercise to do as the manager is to write down what you think your team member's role is and get them to do the same. The chances are that you will agree about most aspects of the role but there will be slight differences in both of your lists. It is in these slight differences where frustration and performance issues can creep in.

This simple exercise enables you to identify areas of potential misunderstanding and where work is required. Over time roles change, so revisiting the role clarity exercise is important. There is nothing more frustrating for a member of staff to find out there has been a misunderstanding about their role at their annual appraisal.

Step 2 – Agree minimum expectations
Where possible goal setting should be a shared exercise and not a top down process. This is particularly important with your high performing staff with whom you should be looking to establish more stretching goals. Establishing the right level of challenge in goals has a direct link to the

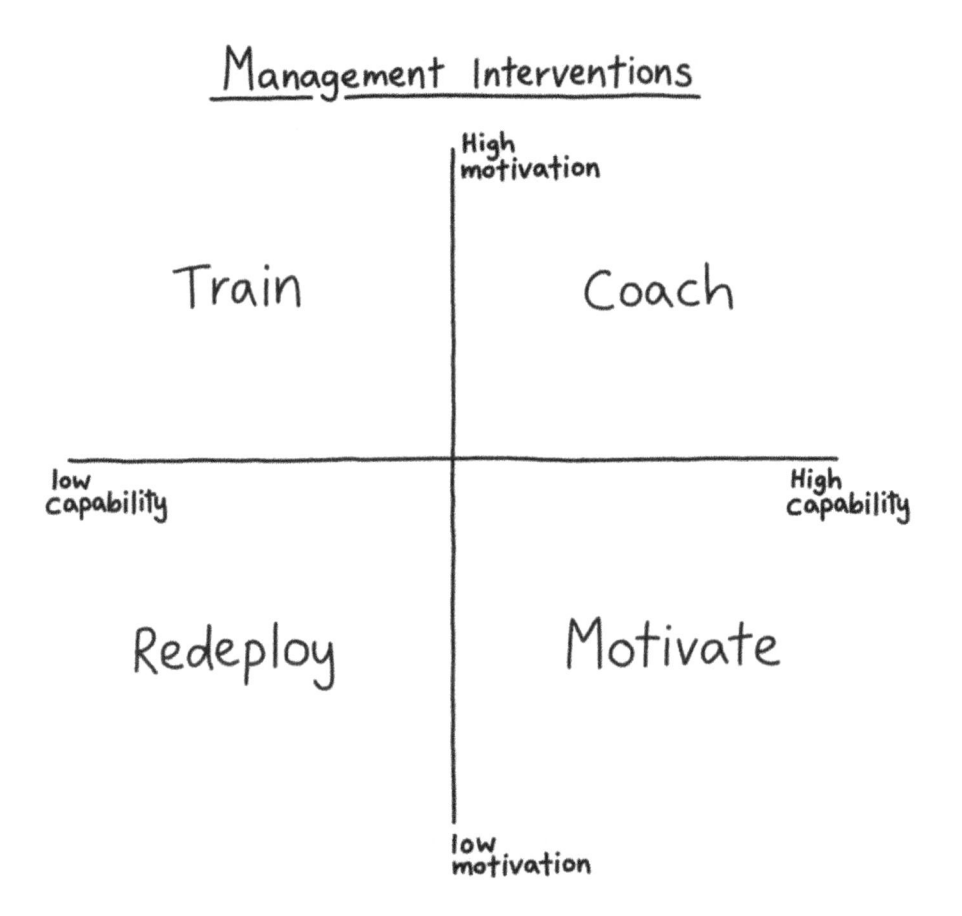

Management Interventions

	High motivation	
Train		Coach
low capability		High capability
Redeploy		Motivate
	low motivation	

motivation of your staff. Too much challenge is demotivating as it feels unachievable. Too little challenge is also demotivating as it feels like there is nothing to strive for.

Steps 3 - Monitor performance and review effectiveness

Tracking performance and making timely interventions are critical in the successful management of performance. Interventions need to be made as soon as performance dips below an agreed level. If this does not happen then a new lower target level is implicitly set. This action can undermine the validity of the original objective setting session. You agreed one thing but in effect a lower level of performance was acceptable. This can set a chain reaction of behaviours that can quickly lead to a rapid decline in performance and standards.

Step 4 – Make appropriate management interventions

Individual performance is built on two factors; capability (can you do the task) and motivation (will you do the task). Any management intervention needs to be tailored in line with these two areas. If someone has low capability but high motivation you should seek to train them. This might be through training courses or other supporting materials but most often this will be done on the job.

If someone has low motivation but high capability you should seek to find ways to re-motivate them. As I have highlighted in other chapters, the best way to do this is by trying to get them to help themselves. This will involve you taking a facilitative approach using questions to uncover the issue and to identify potential ways to rebuild engagement.

If someone has low motivation and low capability you should probably seek to redeploy that member of staff. There is every chance that they are 'a square peg in a round hole' and you should look to find them a role that is more aligned to their core strengths.

If someone has high motivation and high capability you should look to coach them. It is interesting that high performers in the world of sport will nearly always employ a coach to help them take their performance to another level. It's not that the coach can do the role better than them or teach them new things but by using a facilitative approach, can help them unlock hidden potential.

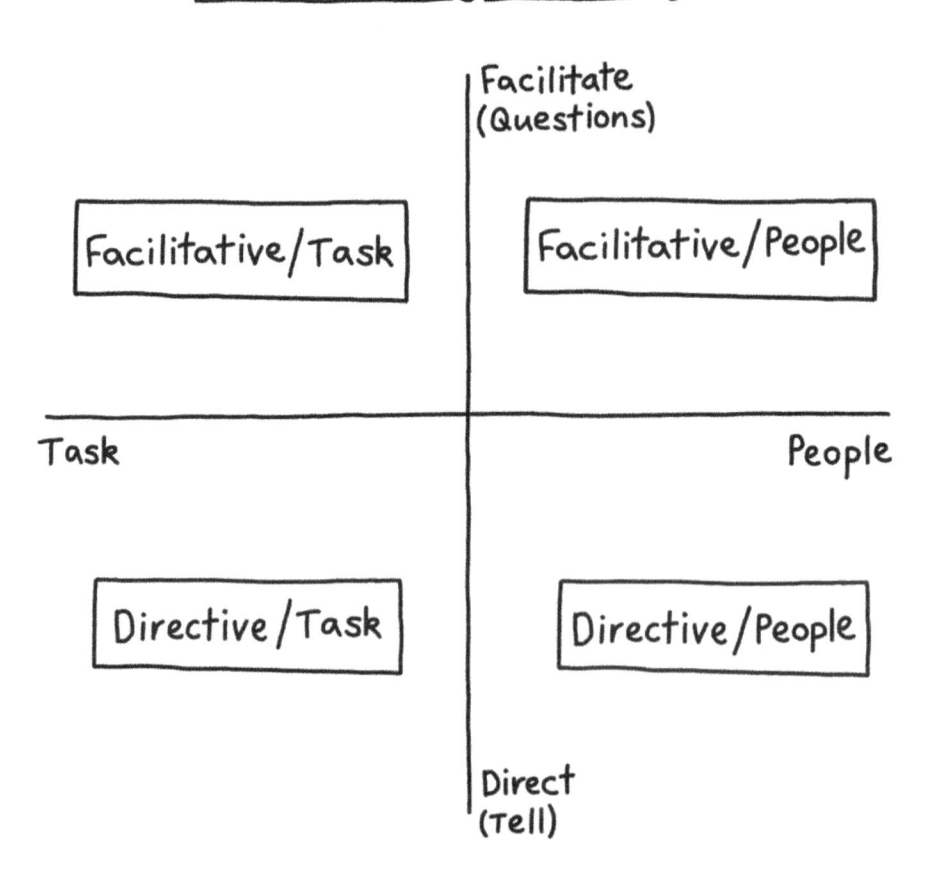

Broad Management Styles

	Facilitate (Questions)	
Facilitative/Task		Facilitative/People
Task		People
Directive/Task		Directive/People
	Direct (Tell)	

Management Basics

Management styles
In addition to managing task, process and people you need to consider your overall management style. We all have preferred ways of working and therefore preferred ways of managing. Your preferred management style might be brilliant in some circumstances but fall well short in others. To be an effective manager you need to be able to flex your approach to the situation that you face.

Your management style comes from a blend of two areas; your focus (do you pay attention to the task or the people) and your approach (do you direct or facilitate). This might give four broad management styles. No one style is best. Different styles are required for different situations. You will find some easier than others.

The Directive/Task Management Style
The directive/task style basically says, 'Do it this way and do it now.' This might be explicitly through direction or implicitly by expecting others to follow your example. It is strongly focussed on task completion and is reinforced by negative, corrective feedback if an individual steps outside of the prescribed way of acting. This style is appropriate for times where specific instruction is required e.g. teaching someone new to a role, working to specific regulatory constraints or times of emergency.

A directive/task style needs to be used sparingly as if overplayed will reduce levels of initiative and engagement in an individual or a team. This can create a negative reinforcing loop i.e. as levels of initiative and engagement drop the need for a directive style increases, and so on. Some managers, with a preference for this style, will seek to make everything urgent or a crisis to justify this approach.

The Facilitative/Task Management Style
The facilitative/task style uses a questioning approach to achieve task completion. In effect you will be leading with questions. It stimulates initiative, after all if you ask a question someone else must think. To adopt this style, you must trust the competence of your people. It works to maxim of, 'We can work this out together.' Examples of when this style may be helpful include working through complex situations where you don't have all the answers, when you are seeking to generate a culture of empowered continuous improvement or working with top performers to bring about further improvement.

Core Coaching Questions

1) Where do you want to be?

2) Where are you now?

3) How will you get there?

4) How does this align to your present work?

Great care needs to be taken in two areas with this style. Firstly it is important to note that when working with a team this style is not looking for a consensus. Most organisations are not democracies and the manager needs to retain their position of authority and the right to have the final decision. If they fail to do this, people may feel that there is no leadership or that there is a lack of clarity about what has been agreed. The second area of caution is in playing with this approach. In this situation, the manager feels that they want to be seen to be non-directive but don't really trust what the individual or the team will come up with. This manifests itself in the use of leading questions or focusing only on the answers that are in line with the manager's view. In this situation people will feel manipulated and levels of trust and engagement will quickly fall.

The Directive/People Management Style
The directive/people style tackles people issues head on. This could include issues like confronting unacceptable individual behaviour, addressing team dynamic issues or offering specific advice to an individual in a mentoring type role. This style does not mean that people will always like what you have to say. Hopefully, if the message is delivered with care, honesty and fairness, people will respect the intervention that you have made. This may be described as, 'tough love', confronting an individual or team with some home truths for their long term benefit.

Many managers avoid using this style, seeking to avoid potential conflict situations or have concerns that they don't have the knowledge or skills to deal with people issues effectively. For example deciding whether someone is operating in line with organisational values can often feel like a subjective judgement open to interpretation. Some managers may also have very low levels of awareness of the people issues going on around them and therefore see little need to use the directive/people style. We have seen though, in this and other chapters, how critical managing the people aspects of your organisation is to overall performance. As such pulling the directive/people style out of your management tool kit, as the situation

The only people who decide whether you are a good manager are the people you manage!

demands, will be integral to your success, no matter how uncomfortable this may feel to you.

The Facilitative/People Management Style
The facilitative/people style focuses on building engagement and buy in at both an individual and a team level. Working with an individual this style could be used to produce clarity for the individual about their own personal aspirations and to seek alignment between their personal journey and that of the organisation. This type of intervention would be framed around three core questions:-
1. Where do you want to be?
2. Where are you now?
3. How will you get there?

Hopefully this will both stimulate their thinking and build their levels of engagement as they recognise the investment that you are making in supporting their own needs. If people see that what they are doing is beneficial to them and the organisation, levels of discretionary effort will increase significantly.

Working with a team this style can be a highly effective way to establish team standards and ways of working. People are much more likely to buy into the 'rules' if they have had the opportunity to shape them themselves. Clive Woodward, in his excellent book 'Winning', demonstrated this approach in how he established a code of conduct with the elite England Rugby Union squad. Without giving up his authority as coach, he got the players to come up with the 'rule book' that they thought was fitting for a team with aspirations to win the rugby world cup. Not only did this ensure full buy in to these ways of operating but also led to the group 'self-policing' how they lived them out. Players would hold each other accountable if behaviour fell below the agreed standards. It is with grudging respect, as a passionate Welsh rugby supporter, that this document proved foundational to England being World Champions in 2003!

Hopefully this chapter has given you some useful insights as to how you can develop as a manager. It's worth remembering the only people who really decide if you are great manager is the people you manage! It's always useful to get their view about how you are doing and where you could improve!

Ideas for Action
Management style feedback
Circulate the simple questionnaire below with members of your team to get feedback on your management style. Do this with care and sensitivity for people's views.

Management Style Feedback Form

Please tick the box which best represents your view of my management style

Directive/Task	Disagree	Somewhat disagree	Somewhat agree	Agree
Regularly gives a lot of direction				
Expects others to follow their example				
Only offers feedback when things go wrong				
Focus is mostly on task completion				
Likes things to be do their way and to their standards				
Facilitative/Task	Disagree	Somewhat disagree	Somewhat agree	Agree
Regularly seeks others ideas how to complete tasks				
Is happy for people to do things their way				
Ensures the team always has an agreed way forward				
Prefers to ask questions than to offer direction				
Encourages people to use their initiative				
Facilitative/People	Disagree	Somewhat disagree	Somewhat agree	Agree
Regularly focus on me and my aspirations				
Uses questions that make me think about my future				
Aligns my needs with the needs of the organisation				
Invests time in my personal development				
Engages the team in establishing standards and values				
Directive/People	Disagree	Somewhat disagree	Somewhat agree	Agree
Offers constructive feedback on my performance				
Praises 5x more than they criticise				
Acts as a mentor to me				
Steps in quickly to address team conflict				
Handles people issues with care, honesty and fairness				

Summary of Management Basics

- As a manager, you need to balance the needs of the task, the process and the people
- Task clarity is critical
- You need a mix of quantitative and qualitative measures to effectively define a task
- SMART goals
    - Specific – What exactly are we trying to achieve?
    - Measurable – How will we know when we have achieved it?
    - Achievable – Is this realistic?
    - Relevance – Why is it important that we achieve this?
    - Timed – When does this need to be achieved by?
- Process improvement
    - Define the area for improvement
    - Analyse the area for improvement
    - Identify root causes – Fishbone analysis and The 5 Whys
    - Generate ideas
    - Implement, review and standardise
- Decide if you need a group or a team
- Team effectiveness framework
    - Goals
    - Processes
    - Roles
    - Relationships
- The four-step performance management process
    - Establish role clarity
    - Agree minimum expectations
    - Monitor performance and review effectiveness
    - Make appropriate management interventions – Train, Motivate, Re-deploy, Coach
- Vary your management style according to the situation
- You are always operating somewhere on the spectrum between tell and asking questions
- You will always be focussing on either the task or the people
- Make sure you don't get locked into one management style

Chapter 9
Three Reasons Why We Don't Delegate

Trust means taking a risk.
Trust is seen in what we do not what we say.

'I've finished the front hedge Dad! Shall I do around the back now?!'

If you ever want to bluff being 'on message', there are several stock words or phrases you can use. Oldies but goodies include 'teamwork', 'communication', 'we need to blue sky this' and 'we need to think outside of the box'. There have been many times that muttering these generalisations got me out of the tricky corner of being caught having a quick nap in the post lunch 'death' session on a course. And I was the trainer! In recent times the buzz words of choice have become 'empowerment' and 'delegation'. Just impart these words with enough gravitas on a management course and just watch the number of sage like nods that you get from your colleagues.

So why is it that people have seen fit to talk more about concepts like empowerment and delegation in recent times? What does it mean to

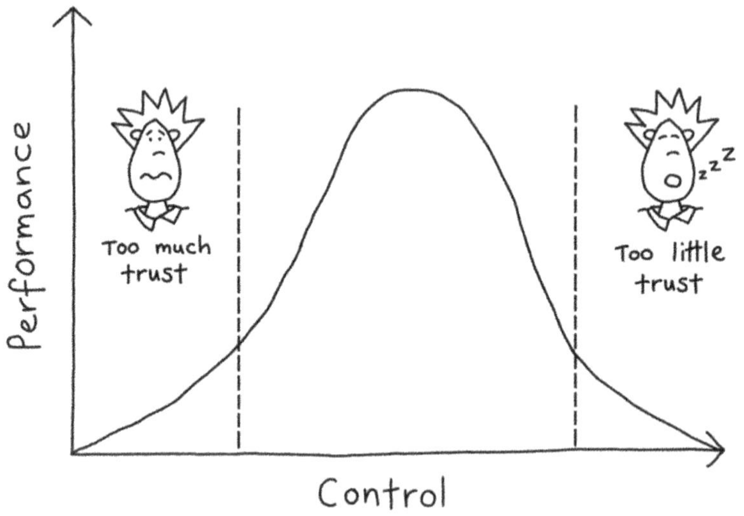
Performance
Too much trust
Too little trust
Control

do these things in practice? Why is it that most managers talk a good game about empowering their staff but seem to keep all the 'power' themselves?

What do we mean by empowerment and delegation?
Empowerment means giving people power. Power can take many forms within an organisation e.g. there is power associated with a position in an organisation. The more senior your position, the more power you are likely to have at your disposal. You can give this power to other people by giving them the authority or permission to act in a certain area. Empowerment might also come from promoting a person to a certain position in the organisation, putting specific resources at their disposal or giving them access to restricted information or knowledge. The big challenge is that empowered people can make a mess of things! This can be damaging to both the organisation and the individuals involved.

Delegation means giving people the authority to act on a specific task or in a given area without the need to refer back. When you are delegating something to somebody, you are saying to them that you are happy to go along with whatever they decide in this area. Clearly this is not something that you should do lightly! It is essential that the person is up to the job and that the area of delegated responsibility is very clearly defined.

Why is empowerment and delegation so important in today's organisations?
Every type of organisation in today's world is continually challenged to deliver more for less. As the biggest cost for most organisations is staff, it is here that the efficiency spotlight most often shines. The senior management in one organisation that I worked seemed to start each year by saying, 'We need to see a 20% reduction in our headcount budget but service standards must stay the same!' By the time that they were saying this for the 6th year in a row I was wondering if there was anyone left or if their cost reduction programme was really delivering what they hoped!

Maximising an individual's performance as a manager comes from finding the sweet spot between trusting your people too little and trusting them too much (see figure over). If you trust someone too little, you will fail to maximise their potential. If trust is misplaced and a person is given too much responsibility i.e. the task is beyond their capability, you run the risk of the job not being done right or not being done at all.

An Outbreak of Common Sense

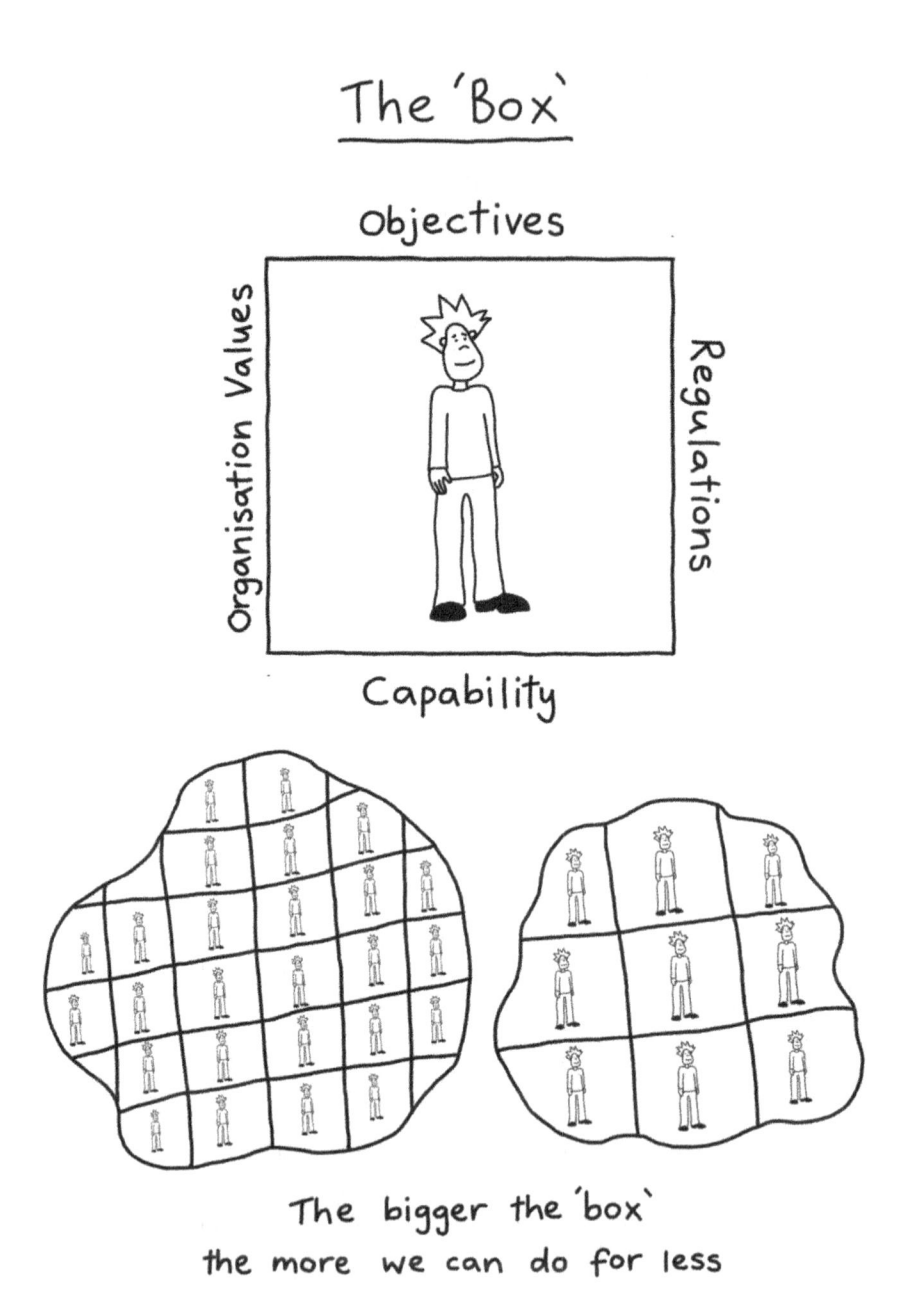

The 'Box'

Objectives

Organisation Values

Regulations

Capability

The bigger the 'box' the more we can do for less

The Box

As I outlined in the chapter on Creating Partners there will always be a 'box' i.e. boundaries within which people must operate. People need to know the boundaries if they are to work to their best e.g. what is my role, what are my objectives, what am I allowed to do, what resources do I have, how do things work around here, what's legal, what's acceptable etc. Lack of clarity is disconcerting. If people are disconcerted they will become more averse to taking risks or taking on increased responsibility.

Empowerment and delegation gives people a bigger 'box' in which to operate. As people become comfortable using their discretion more, levels of engagement and initiative will increase. Not only does this feel good to the individual but your organisation will also benefit as levels of discretionary effort increase. This will help in achieving more for less. Also, the flexibility/responsiveness of your organisation will improve as staff become less constrained and more prepared to use their initiative to respond to the issue in hand.

Why is empowerment and delegation difficult to do?
It is easy to talk a good game about empowerment and delegation. One manager I used to work for in the bank used to drive me potty by doing this. He would regularly give me the responsibility for dealing with a customer request or complaint but then ask me to 'quickly run my response by him' before it was sent out. This invariably led him to a complete rewrite of what I had done. I used to question why he had ever asked me to do it in the first place; it seemed a complete waste of my time. I wonder how often I have been guilty of doing the same thing with people I have managed. I believe that there are three fundamental reasons why we find empowerment and delegation difficult to do in practice.

Reason #1 – The difference between accountability and responsibility

I feel at this point that I must confess to being one of the founder members of the World's Worst Delegators Club. I really am rubbish at delegation; a few years ago, I had my first real insight as to why this is the case. One day I was working in my garden when one of my daughters asked me if she could use the electric hedge trimmer to cut the front hedge. My answer was immediately no but why do you think that was? Well, all of you great parents out there will probably be thinking that it was because I was worried about the welfare of my daughter; she might hurt herself with this powerful

Accountability

Leader — Has the task been done?!

⬇

Responsibility

Team member — Do the task

tool. I wish that had been my first thought, I would feel a whole lot better about myself as a father. No, my prime reason for saying no was because I was worried about the 'welfare' of my hedge. She could hack it to death in seconds!! Then picture the scene; my wife returns home from work and sees a devastated front hedge or even worse, because she is a good parent, a daughter minus a limb! Who do you think that she might hold accountable for this?! It certainly wouldn't work if I tried to plead my case by saying that it was my daughters fault, after all she had been the one responsible for the devastation.

This incident brought into sharp focus the first reason I find it so hard to delegate. When you delegate something, you give the responsibility to complete a task to the other person but you retain the ultimate accountability for the outcome. In organisational life, this dynamic is continually playing out. If it is your neck on the block your natural inclination will be to keep control and trust less. This gets worse the more the stakes rise. Giving my daughter control of the hedge trimmer could quickly have led to a disastrous outcome. The fact was I didn't trust her with this power, especially as I was the one accountable for the outcome.

Reason #2 - 'It will be done better if I do it myself'

The second reason why we commonly have a problem letting go is the mindset, 'It will be done better if I do it myself'. Again, this can be illustrated with a domestic example. One domain of mine at home is the washing up. I quite enjoy washing up if I am left on my own and can listen to my choice of radio programme or podcast. I am a stickler for the washing up water being hot, after all that is the only way that you can guarantee things are clean. When one of my girls has washed up I can't help myself testing the temperature of the water that they have used. Again, it's confession time. There have been occasions that if I don't think the water they have used has been hot enough, I will redo it after they have gone! I think that perhaps I need counselling.

The belief, 'It will be done better if I do it myself' is also highly prevalent in organisational life. There is a fair chance that this statement may be right. If you have been given a management position you probably have been very good at the tasks that your team members should now be doing. You may well be the most skilled person in the team. However, if you fail to let go there will be a number of consequences: -

An Outbreak of Common Sense

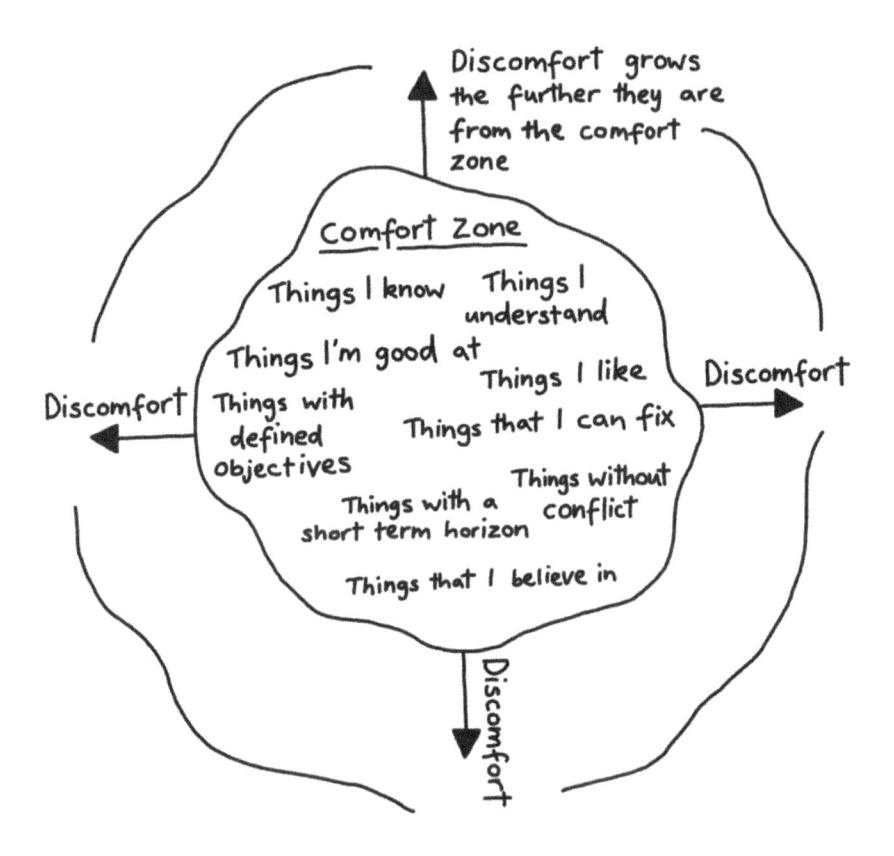

The Comfort Zone

Comfort Zone
- Things I know
- Things I understand
- Things I'm good at
- Things I like
- Things with defined objectives
- Things that I can fix
- Things with a short term horizon
- Things without conflict
- Things that I believe in

Discomfort grows the further they are from the comfort zone

Discomfort ← Discomfort → Discomfort ↓

- You will become bogged down with work
- You will fail to do the management tasks that you should be freeing yourself up to do
- You will annoy and frustrate your team
- You will fail to develop your team
- You will breed reliance on you doing everything

The prime reason that we fall into the 'It will be done better if I do it myself' trap is standards. The standards that you prefer to work to may far exceed what is required for the job and be beyond the capability of your team. In this nothing anyone else does is good enough or as good as it could have been if you did it. Having high standards is not a bad thing but if the bar is set so high that only you can clear it, this will create problems within your team.

Reason #3 - The comfort zone

The third reason that we may have a problem letting go is that we just don't want to let go! Two strong drivers for human beings are to follow the easiest path (thereby conserving energy) and to do things that make us feel good. Following these two drivers leads you to stick to jobs that you know, that you can do well and that give you a buzz. There are some tasks you just don't want to let go of because they sit fair and square within your comfort zone and you like them too much.

Clarity may be one of the reasons why a task sits within our comfort zone. The clearer a task is i.e. the more we know what needs to be done and by when, the more it sits within our comfort zone. Often the team's tasks are clearer than the vaguer stuff of effective management and leadership that we are supposed to be doing e.g. strategic thinking, forecasting, trying to make change happen etc. In this case, you may not want to delegate the clearer tasks because you are looking for a good excuse to avoid doing the ambiguous things that you dislike!

Another common reason for staying within our comfort zone is that we like to feel important and indispensable; it makes us feel good. This can tie in with a 'hero' mindset of leadership i.e. the situation demands that I roll my sleeves up and dive into the task to rescue things. I have worked with leaders who try to make everything a crisis to justify why they are always involved in the task rather than stepping back to be a more effective in their role. Asking people to do things can also be awkward and place you outside of your comfort zone. You may feel bad about adding to their

Delegation is a 2 way process

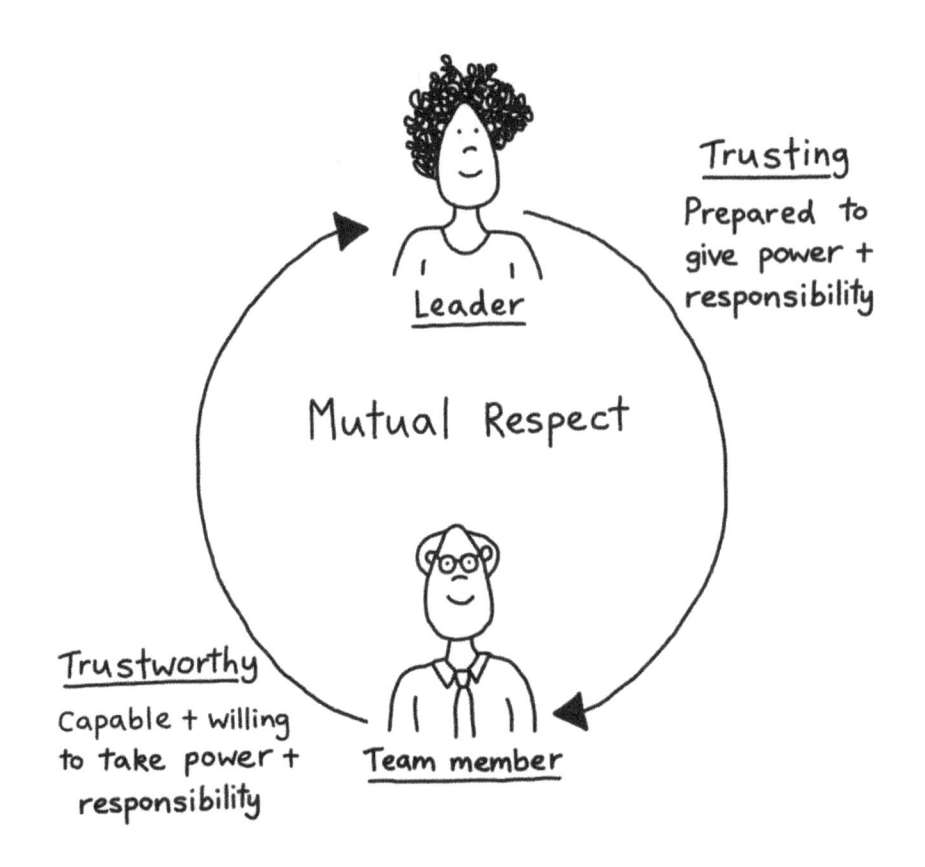

Leader

Mutual Respect

Team member

Trusting
Prepared to give power + responsibility

Trustworthy
Capable + willing to take power + responsibility

workload or asking them to do difficult things. It may require you to have to exert influence or authority in a given situation which may feel uncomfortable to you.

All these things can push you into the potential trap of saying, 'It's just easier if I do it myself'. If you critically examine how you spend your time it's amazing how often you drift back to the things that are in your comfort zone. As you take positions of increased authority within an organisation, these are the very tasks that you should be delegating.

How we justify not delegating

The combination of these three powerful factors can lead us to hold on to far too much. Often, we are aware of this and don't feel very comfortable about it. Leaders who know that they should be letting go of more, go through a whole array of mental gymnastics to justify their actions. Common excuses include: -

- It's just this time
- I don't have the time to train people up
- I don't want to over burden my team
- I don't have anyone to delegate to
- I should lead by example and be seen mucking in

There will be an element of truth in these excuses; however, you should not allow this to stop you from tackling the challenge of effectively empowering your team. The amount of time that you have in a day is finite and how you spend it is always down to a matter of choice. You need to constantly guard against the fact that you are justifying your actions in holding on to certain tasks. As someone reminded me the other day, if you are saying 'yes' to one thing then you must be saying 'no' to something else. The things that we are saying no to are often the proactive tasks of leadership, that if done well, will develop a healthier, more sustainable and effective organisation.

Delegation is a two-way process

The recent trend to promote empowerment and delegation has predominately focussed on getting managers to give over power and responsibility to their teams. This though is only one side of the empowerment story. For empowerment to happen the person being empowered must also want to take on the responsibility in this area. With power comes responsibility. People don't always want to be trusted with this responsibility.

An Outbreak of Common Sense

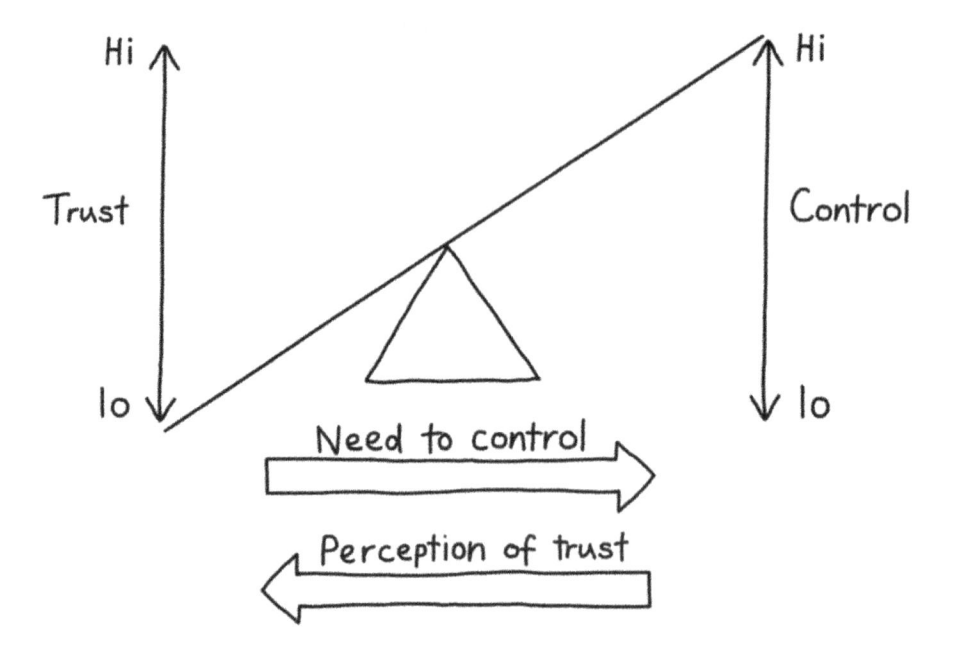

Hi ↑   ↑ Hi
Trust   Control
lo ↓   ↓ lo

Need to control →
← Perception of trust

We spend a lot of time sending people on leadership courses to encourage them to delegate more but what do we do for those who will be delegated to? I sometimes liken this to sending all husbands away on an effective marriage course and then returning them, all keen and enthusiastic, to their wives with the message of how things will be different for their relationship going forward. I don't know about you but I know how my wife would respond to that!

Picture the scene of the eager manager returning from their course telling their team that they are now going to empower them more. For 'empower me more' many of the team will read 'dump more on me, more like!' Being trusted by your boss to take on more responsibility can be extremely motivating. However, the challenge must feel manageable. I'm sure that we have all experienced the odd 'sphincter tightening moment' when we have felt out of our depth in a particular situation or doing a certain task at work!

The trust see-saw

Another perspective of the two-way nature of empowerment and delegation is the trust see-saw. From the manager's viewpoint, we look at this from left to right; as trust in the team member goes up and down so does the manager's need for control; low trust leads to high control, high trust leads to low control. From the team member's viewpoint, we look at the model from right to left; as their perception of how much they are being controlled by their manager goes up and down, so does their perception of how much they feel they are trusted by the manager; high control means I'm not trusted, low control means I am trusted.

We have already seen that it is very easy for managers to retain too much control and not trust their staff enough. This can easily set up a negative spiral in which your team feel less trusted and disengage, which in turn encourages the manager to take more control. I have commonly worked with managers who have said that they don't have staff who they could delegate to. My first thought when they say this is, 'What has the manager been doing that has created this potentially self-fulfilling negative dynamic!'

A manager's beliefs

I believe the single biggest factor that limits the performance of an individual is the belief that their manager has in them. Our beliefs are formed as we make sense of our experiences and then project these forward into the

The Belief Cycle

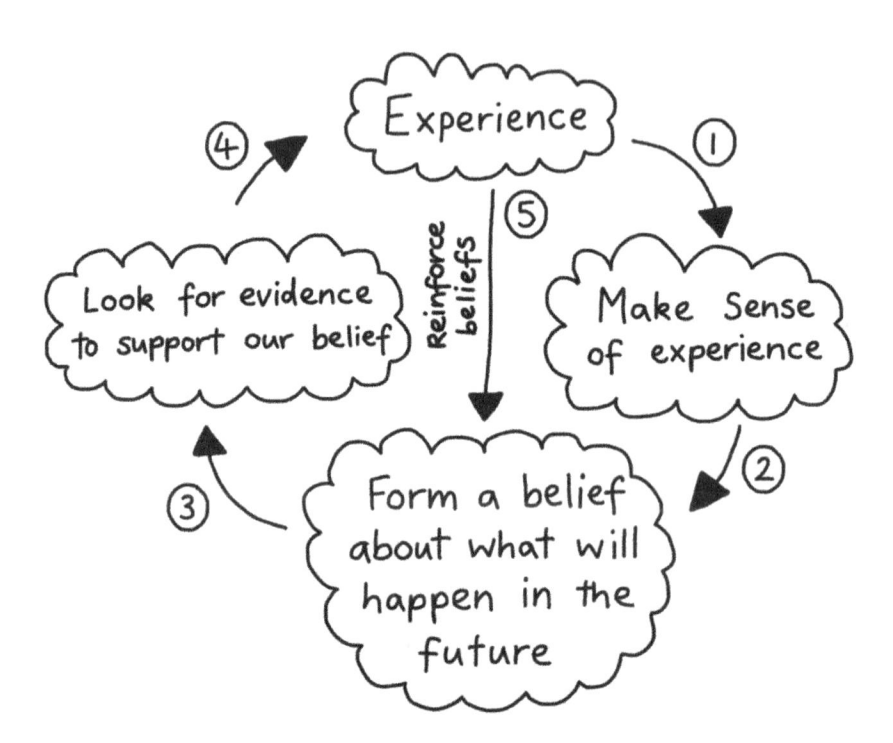

- Experience
- Make Sense of experience
- Form a belief about what will happen in the future
- Look for evidence to support our belief
- Reinforce beliefs

① Experience → Make Sense of experience
② Make Sense of experience → Form a belief about what will happen in the future
③ Form a belief → Look for evidence to support our belief
④ Look for evidence → Experience
⑤ Reinforce beliefs

future as a map of what we expect to happen. The cycle of how we form and reinforce our beliefs is shown over. The more positive the experience a manager has of a team member, the more positively they will believe in them. However, once we have formed a belief our brains become biased in looking for information to support that belief e.g. if you have low levels of belief in a member of staff, you will be more likely to notice the things that they do wrong in the future.

I have lost count of the number of times that I have seen a member of staff perform very poorly with one manager, only to become a star when they have been transferred to another manager with different experiences/beliefs about them. Beliefs can be contagious. If you tell another manager that someone is a 'waste of space' then they will immediately be put on their guard and start to notice all the negative things about that person's behaviour. I used to work with a training manager who always wanted to brief me about all the delegates that I was about to have on my courses. This was particularly biased to trying to tell me which ones that I should look out for! Whilst his intentions were good, I didn't want to know as I knew that it would immediately colour my judgement of the group.

If your beliefs might be limiting your staff's performance it is common sense that you should continually challenge yourself to test the validity of your thinking. A danger when doing this is that you just seek to justify your thinking, only sorting for the evidence that backs up your judgement. To effectively test the assumptions you are working to, it is often helpful to enlist the support of someone who can act as a 'critical friend'. Key questions that might help in this include: -

- How much do you really trust this individual?
- How does your trust in them vary in different tasks and situations?
- How have you come to these judgements? What have you noticed or heard?
- What might you be missing about them?
- If you have a lack of trust, is this an issue of their capability or their will?
- What would they have to do or demonstrate for you to trust them more?
- How clear have you been about setting boundaries for them?
- Have you ever talked to them about this?!

World's Worst Delegators Club

Application form

I the undersigned agree to :-

- Hold on to as much as I can
- Hold on to the things I enjoy doing
- Work to the belief that no none can do a task as well as I can do it
- Never take the risk of trusting others for tasks which am accountable
- Always justify my actions

Print name _____ Signed x _____

How to delegate and empower more
Here are some ideas to help you to delegate and empower more.

Develop the trustworthiness and willingness of your staff to take on more responsibility.
Consider what you are doing to develop their capability; what training are you offering, what opportunities are you giving them to develop on the job? Seek to build their confidence; offer positive feedback, catch them doing things right, help them recognise what their potential may be. Reward people who use their initiative; this doesn't just have to be financial, give people interesting opportunities, praise, access to further development opportunities.

Build trust through a series of small steps
It is probably best for both parties to build trust through a series of small steps. Agree the step of increased responsibility, review how this worked out, reflect on the learning and then agree the next step forward. It is worth remembering that once trust has been established it must be guarded carefully. It is often said that it can take years to build trust but that it can be destroyed in a second! If someone is hurt by your actions, it will take a lot for them to trust you again.

Define clear boundaries
The clearer people are as to the boundaries within which they can use their discretion, the more likely they are to exercise this authority. Be very clear about what is being delegated and the limits of the power being given. Ensure these boundaries are acceptable to both the you and your team member.

Stick with it!
Building a culture of delegation and empowerment within your team requires real discipline and perseverance. In the madness of everyday work life, it is all too easy to work on autopilot and fail to examine your actions and thinking as a manager, and to consider the impact these are having on the performance of your team.

Are you going to do something about it or should I send you the application form to join me in the World's Worst Delegators Club!?

Ideas for Action
Create a learning group
One of the best ways to gain new perspectives and to reflect on your own actions is to create a learning group. A learning group should comprise of around 4-6 people and you should aim to meet for 2-3 hours once a quarter. The learning group provides a forum to explore the different management challenges everyone is facing. It is often helpful to follow a structure when exploring an issue to avoid it becoming an unfocussed talking shop. One approach I have found helpful is as follows: -

- One person shares their issue with the group (2-3 minutes)
- The group ask questions to clarify their understanding of the issue (5 minutes)
- The person then goes and sits in another part of the room away from the group
- The remaining group discuss how they might approach the issue whilst the person listens and takes notes (10 minutes)
- The person then returns to the group and then summarises what insights they have gained and what they will do differently (5 minutes)

You can see that the whole process, exploring one person's issue, should take no longer than half an hour. Whilst any management issue could be explored it may be helpful, within the context of this chapter, to dedicate one session to issues around delegation and how you might improve in this area.

Personal challenge
Take some time out to reflect on what it would take for you to delegate more to each member of your team.

- What work could you pass over?
- What do you think that you must hold on to?
- What is the basis for your judgements in these areas?
- How are you justifying your decisions?
- What would have to be true for you to act differently?
- What are the consequences of you choosing to hold on to the things you are?
- Are you prepared to try to delegate more to this individual?
- What conversation do you need to make this happen?

Summary of three reasons why we don't delegate
- Empowerment means giving people with power. With that power, they might make mistakes.
- Delegation means giving a person the power to act in a given area without the need for further recall to you
- If we are to achieve more for less we must be prepared to empower our staff and delegate key responsibilities and tasks
- Delegation is easier said than done. It is all to easy to talk a good game about delegation but to fail to do it in action
- Factors that stop us delegating include: -
    o The difference between accountability and responsibility
    o A belief that we can do the job better ourselves
    o A desire to stay in our comfort zone
- The belief a manager has in the capability of a team member will have a significant impact on their performance
- We need to continually test the validity of the judgements on which we are basing our decision whether to delegate
- Don't join me in the World's Worst Delegators Club!

Chapter 10
Personal Effectiveness

To be effective, we must have balance in our lives

Dave didn't know what was worse, the backache or the earache for refusing to see a doctor!

The first step to being an effective leader or manager is being able to manage yourself. So, there I was working as a business banking manager, happily chatting to a customer about how his business was going, when suddenly everything started to go black. For those of you old enough to remember, it was like switching off an early television, my sight started to close in and the customer was left as a tiny speck in the centre of my vision. I can still remember thinking, 'Oh no what a place to die, the blinking interview room of Watford branch!'

I was scared. I didn't know what to do, so I just sat there. After a couple of minutes, which seemed like an eternity, everything returned to normal. I don't know what it says about my interpersonal skills but the customer seemed to be completely oblivious of anything untoward going on! I finished the meeting and decided to go and get some fresh air. My legs felt like ten tonne weights and I could hardly put one foot in front of the other. Now even though I am a man and, as we know, men don't do doctors, I knew something was up that demanded a visit to my GP. Up until that point I had thought stress was just an excuse to get out of work.

Importance

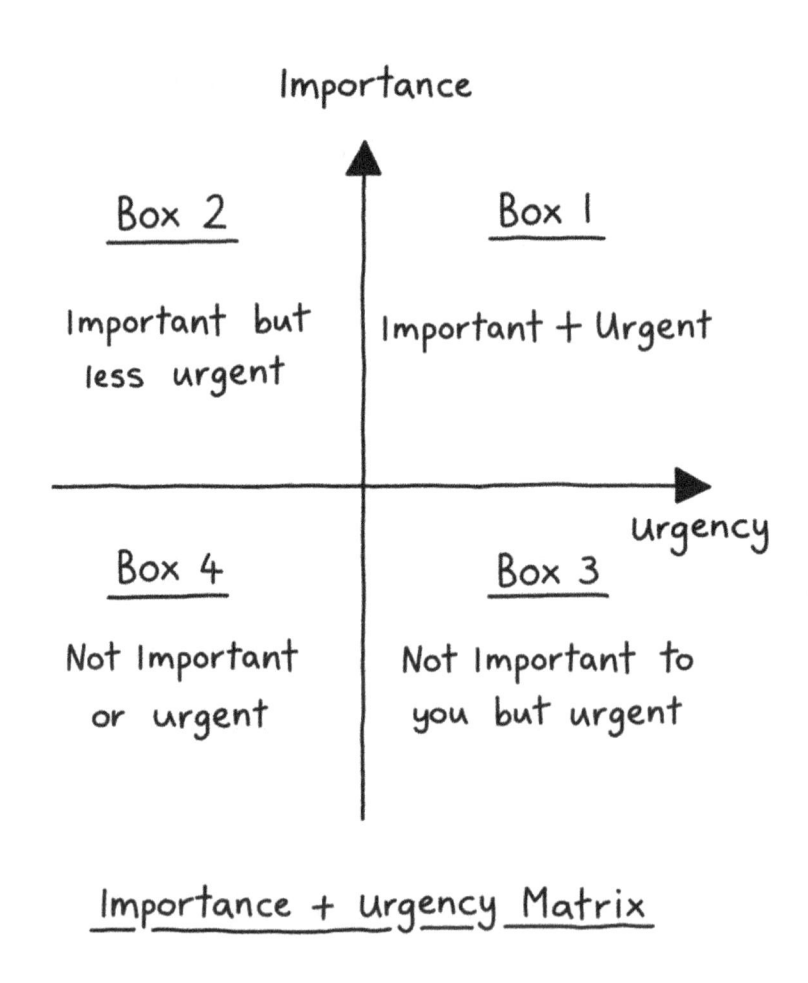

Box 2	Box 1
Important but less urgent	Important + Urgent
Box 4	Box 3
Not Important or urgent	Not Important to you but urgent

urgency →

Importance + urgency Matrix

I had everything under control, that sort of thing would never affect me. My GP had a different view! 'You are suffering from stress, your blood pressure is sky high and if you carry on this way you will knock at least 20 years off your life', he happily told me. 'I suggest that you do something about it!'

This was a genuine surprise to me. I knew that there had been a lot on my plate in recent times but I thought that I had been coping with it ok. I had been ignoring the warning signs such as tiredness, irritability, unexpected moments of anxiety and working longer hours but not achieving more. I had been too busy 'doing' to notice that things were slowly but surely coming off the rails. It really is common sense; if we don't have balance in our lives we will become increasingly ineffective. It's a bit like running a car and never having it serviced. If we don't take time to look after ourselves it will come back to bite us.

I had to make some changes. I set strict start and finish times for my working day to ensure that I had time for my young family. I took a lunch hour every day and used that time, three days a week, to go swimming. Not only would this improve my state of health but also no one could call me whilst I was underwater! And then a surprising thing happened. Even though I was working shorter hours my performance improved, so much so in fact that I became one of the top performers in my area. It was somewhat ironic that I achieved more by working less! It was then that I learnt what matters is not the number of hours we work but how effective we are that matters.

Importance and Urgency
One of the things that is absolutely fixed in life is the number of hours that you have in a day. Your personal effectiveness will be governed by how you choose to use this time. Everything that you do on any given day can be rated against two criteria; importance and urgency. We can use these two criteria to make a simple matrix (see over page).

If you were looking at how you should prioritise your day, then Box 1 tasks (important and urgent) should be the things that you do first. There is often a bit of a debate about what you should do next. We should do Box 2 (important but less urgent tasks) but we often end up going to Box 3 next. Box 3 tasks are not important to you but often are to someone else, who is probably pressuring you to get them done now. Box 4 (Not important and not urgent) tasks are the lowest priority.

Important

Box 2
- Proactive activities
- Stepping back, slower paced
- Benefits take time to be seen
- Can be ambiguous + difficult to track
- Platform for future success

Box 1
- Reactive activities
- Adrenalin fueled, fast paced
- Quick hits
- Clearly defined and measurable
- Stressful + self defeating

Box 4
- Activities can be a therapeutic counter balance to a mad Box 1 world

Box 3
- Activities are based around pleasing others
- Saying 'No' may create tension and conflict

Urgent →

The nature of the four boxes
   Box 1

Well that's all well and good as a bit of time management theory but most days, we never get out of Box 1! Box 1 is full of those things that just must be done today. We might start the day with a plan but this disappears out of the window as our time becomes consumed by random, unscheduled Box 1 activities. The demands of Box 1 seem to have grown with the increasing development of electronic communication media. There seems to be no escape from the urgent demands of work.

At another level, Box 1 can be addictive. Box 1 activities are adrenalin fuelled. Working under pressure can be a buzz; it's down to you to get things done and it's important that you succeed. Box 1 activities are often very clearly defined. You will know exactly what must be done and by when. We will always favour activities that are clear over those which are ambiguous. Completing tasks also makes us feel good. Another confession; on some days when I have done something that wasn't on my 'to do' list, I have written it on my list after I have done it, just so I can tick it off. I know that I am not alone in this!

It doesn't take a rocket scientist to work out what happens to effectiveness if we remain for extended periods in Box 1. We all need a bit of challenge in a day to get motivated but remaining in Box 1, as my story illustrates, leads to stress and an increasing decline in performance.

Box 3

I know I have jumped Box 2 but I want to leave that until last. We need to accept that there will always be occasions when we will need to put our agenda to one side, stop what we are doing and do things for the benefit of someone else. In many ways being prepared to work this way is foundational to operating effectively in any group or team. However, if our time becomes full of Box 3 activities we will fail to achieve what we need to do. This means that occasionally we will need to say 'no' to other people's demands.

Saying 'no' though can often feel very uncomfortable. We like to be liked and saying 'no' to someone might seem to put this under threat. We also tend to try to steer clear of conflict and often feel that saying 'yes' to other people's requests will give us an easier life. If we are to remain personally effective, we must develop the ability to say 'no' at the right time and in a manner, that causes the least upset.

Physician, heal thyself!

So, I teach this stuff about personal effectiveness, my life will be sorted, right? If only that were true. Maintaining a Box 2 balance is a challenge for all of us. Here are some examples of how the Box 1 trap bites me.

Business Development

The Box 2 activity, business development, is my Achilles heel. I really hate networking and seeking to promote myself. I work predominately on my own and at any time will have an in-depth relationship with a small group of clients. This often means that my diary will have intensive periods of Box 1 activities, including extensive travel, as I work with a leader and their team/organisation as they seek to navigate a fundamental period of change.

The combination of these intense periods of busyness and my inherent dislike of business development activities often means that I will put this work off. The impact on my business of failing to do this Box 2 activity is that the flow of my work/income becomes very lumpy; times of relative feast being followed by times of relative famine as I seek to find the next pieces of work.

Personal Development

Unlike business development, I really enjoy the Box 2 activity of personal development. Not only do I find this intellectually stimulating but as with many service industries my product is me. Continued personal development is therefore critical in continuing to develop my service offering.

So why might I find it difficult to keep up a steady flow of personal development activities? Well the truth is, when I fall into the Box 1 trap I often feel too mentally tired to engage with it. This can create a downward cycle as the lack of stimulation from personal development leaves me feeling increasingly jaded.

Keeping fit

Regular exercise and maintaining a healthy diet are a continual challenge to me. It's easy for me to justify why I don't do this as I travel the world but failing to sort this regularly comes back to bite me. I know the theory but it's a battle putting it into practice!

Box 4

You might ask why anybody might spend any time in Box 4 on activities that are neither important nor urgent. Well this comes down to the fact that we are not just logic driven machines that make decisions on how we spend our time just on an economic cost/benefit analysis. The people who design video games and mobile phone game apps seem to understand this completely. Come on; own up, what has been your guilty secret of a time-wasting game that has become a near addiction! For me saving the world from a plague of evil pigs by flinging a range of angry birds at them seemed to become unhealthily important for a time.

When our world becomes dominated by important and urgent demands we can often find a form of therapeutic release in Box 4 activities. However, whilst the distraction of Box 4 activities may be attractive, clearly staying here for extended periods will not be helpful to you.

Box 2

Box 2 activities are the proactive tasks which will bring sustained improvement to your effectiveness and performance. Examples of Box 2 activities are: -

- Developing capability and capacity to deliver
- Prevention
- Working out strategies and plans
- Personal reflection
- Reviewing outcomes and approaches
- Root cause analysis of issues
- Innovation
- Clarifying goals
- Developing relationships
- Maintaining health e.g. exercise, sleep, life balance

Whilst this type of activities is not perceived to be urgent, if you fail to do them it will cause you problems. It can be said that the problems you are experiencing today are down to the Box 2 activities that you failed to do yesterday. There will always be activities in your day that fall into each of the four boxes. The key to getting ahead of the game is to achieve a better Box 2 balance and in breaking free from the potential Box 1 trap, where everything seems to be both important and urgent.

Balanced Goal Setting

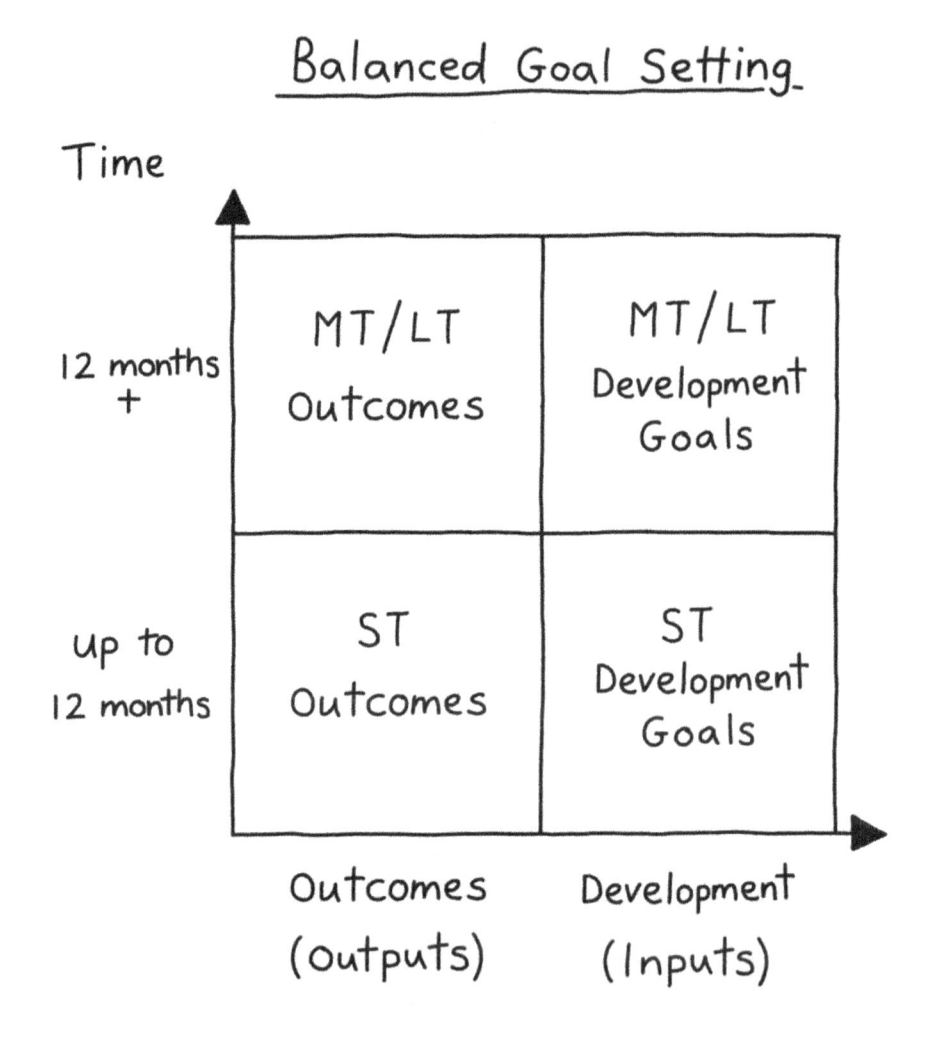

	Outcomes (outputs)	Development (Inputs)
12 months +	MT/LT Outcomes	MT/LT Development Goals
up to 12 months	ST Outcomes	ST Development Goals

Time ↑

Breaking free from the 'Box 1' trap
We can see that it is easy to fall into the trap of having a life dominated by important and urgent tasks. Prolonged periods of this will be damaging. Breaking free of the Box 1 trap requires discipline and determination and achieving a better balance between Box 1 and Box 2 activities needs to be continually revisited. Detailed below are some practical hints and tips for doing this.

Be clear about what is important
It may seem stupid but we are often not clear about what really is important to us. If something is important there will be a clear link to this activity contributing to your core purpose and top level goals. The clearer you are about purpose and goals the easier you will find it to make decisions about what you should be filling your diary with.

- Purpose – What are the things that give your life purpose?
- Top level goals – What do you want to achieve in the short, medium and long term?

This fantastic quote from Stephen Covey brings this into sharp focus, 'You have to decide what your highest priorities are and have the courage, pleasantly, smilingly, non-apologetically, to say "no" to other things. And the way you do that is by having a bigger "yes" burning inside.'

Create specific goals for Box 2 activities
Broadly speaking you should have goals in two areas; Outcomes – what you want to achieve and Development Goals – what needs to be put in place to achieve your desired outcomes. For many years during my banking career I wanted to become a trainer but as each year passed by I got no closer to achieving this. I had no development goals in place. After attending a course that highlighted this fact, I made an appointment to meet with the Regional Training Manager. I asked him what I would have to do to be considered for a training role. He highlighted several areas including skills development and relevant experience. These became my development goals. Within 18 months I secured my dream role.

In many ways, the development goals are the most important. It is by achieving these that you increase your chances of delivering your desired outcomes. As the golfer, Gary Player once said, 'The more I practice, the luckier I get!' The practice embodied his development goals.

The Rocks in a Jar

So the story is told, a university professor was addressing his class of students at the start of their degree course about how best they should manage their time. To illustrate his talk, he placed a large glass jar on the table in front of him and told the group that the jar represented the finite amount of time available to them. He then placed several large rocks into the jar. He turned to his students and asked, 'Is the jar full?'

One of the students replied, 'Yes, it's full of rocks.'

We'll see', said the professor. He then got a bag of gravel and poured it into the jar. The gravel worked its way around the large rocks. When the jar could take no more gravel he asked the group again, 'Is the jar full?'

Another student replied, 'Yes, it's definitely full now.'

We'll see', said the professor. He then got a bag of sand and repeated what he had done with the gravel. Again, he asked, 'Is the jar full?'

The students were now much less sure of themselves. No one seemed to be bold enough to offer a view. 'Well let's see', said the professor. He then got a jug of water and slowly filled the jar until the water started to leak over the edges. 'I think that we can all agree that this is now a full jar', said the professor as he mopped up the excess water on the table. 'So, what can this illustration tell us about how you might manage your time this year?' he asked the group.

After a little time one of the students tentatively raised their hand. 'I think that it tells us that no matter how busy we think that we might be, there is always the space to squeeze something else in.'

'An interesting thought', said the professor, 'but one that I fear that will lead you to have a very unhappy year. No, the thing that this illustration tells us is make sure that you put the big rocks in first! Know what is really important to you and then fit everything else around that.'

Build your diary around your Box 2 Activities

There will always be something that will fill your day. If your diary is already full of Box 1 activities, you will never find the space for a Box 2 activity. Take for example attending a training course. Could you, this week, find the time to attend a 1 day training course? The chances are you wouldn't be able to do this. How far ahead would you have to go before you could find a full day free for training – a month or more? If you did book this training day, then other Box 1 activities would have to fit in around it e.g. you may need to say to your customers that you would be unavailable for calls that day. Given sufficient notice most people are ok with this.

The principle here is to control your diary. If you look far enough ahead, you can put the Box 2 activities in first and then manage the busyness of Box 1 around them. This principle is well illustrated by the often told story of the Rocks in The Jar (see over). Exactly what Box 2 activities you should be placing in your diary is covered by the next tip.

Turn Box 2 activities into specific actions

One of the factors that make it more difficult to action Box 2 activities is that they are difficult to define. Take for example the classic Box 2 activity of development. Development can cover a huge variety of areas and different approaches, what exactly are we supposed to be doing? If you are going to effectively diarise Box 2 activities, you need to drill down and make them more specific. For example, looking at development, the following questions might help to sharpen your focus:

- What are your key objectives?
- What capabilities would you need to have to achieve these?
- Where are you against this defined group of capabilities?
- What are the specific development gaps/priorities?
- What development activities might you need to put in place to fill these gaps?
- How will you know that these development activities have been successful?
- What are you presently not doing that would have the biggest impact on you achieving your goals?' This question has the habit of shining the light on the Box 2 activity that we have been trying to avoid!

Breaking the Box 1 Trap

1) Be clear about what's important
2) Create specific goals for Box 2 activities
3) Build your diary around Box 2 activities
4) Turn Box 2 activities into specific actions
5) Commit to Box 2 activities
6) Don't mix Box 1 + Box 2 activities and time
7) Schedule regular time to review your Box 1/Box 2 balance

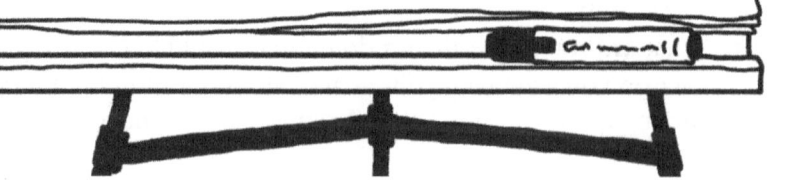

Commit to Box 2 activities

If you make a prior commitment to do a proactive, Box 2 task, the likelihood of you doing this task will go up significantly. For example, take the Box 2 activity of keeping fit. If you commit to going to the gym tonight at a specific time you are much more likely to do this when the time comes. The decision has already been made in your mind.

You can increase the likelihood of following through on Box 2 activities still further if you publicly commit to the activity or ask other people to hold you to account for doing it. One of the reasons that having regular coaching sessions is so helpful is that you know that you must report back to your coach on whether you have followed through on your commitments. No one likes to go into that follow up conversation with nothing to report!

Don't mix Box 1 and Box 2 activities and time

The character and nature of Box 1 and Box 2 activities are completely different. Box 1 is frenetic and has a short-term focus. Box 2 requires space and time. I often say to leadership teams seeking to work on Box 2 activities, you need to allow time for 'your wheels to spin for a bit' before you really start to get some traction and make progress. You can't just say, 'I need a strategy for this organisation and I need it now!' Box 2 doesn't work like this.

If you don't create space for Box 2 activities the Box 1 agenda will dominate your time and thinking. You need to schedule specific time away from the operational agenda for Box 2 activities and you need to guard that time ferociously against operational issues sneaking on to the agenda.

Schedule regular time to reflect on your Box 1/Box 2 balance

Breaking out of the Box 1 trap requires real determination. The incessant challenges thrown at you in a fast-moving world will always mean that you will be in danger of falling back into the trap. The issue is not about losing your balance but how quickly you get it back again. For this reason, you need to schedule time at specific intervals to reflect on your balance both individually and organisationally and take the appropriate steps to make sure you remain on track.

It's not easy to break out of the Box 1 trap but as my Dad used to say, 'Any old jelly fish can go with the flow; it takes something with a backbone to swim against it'!

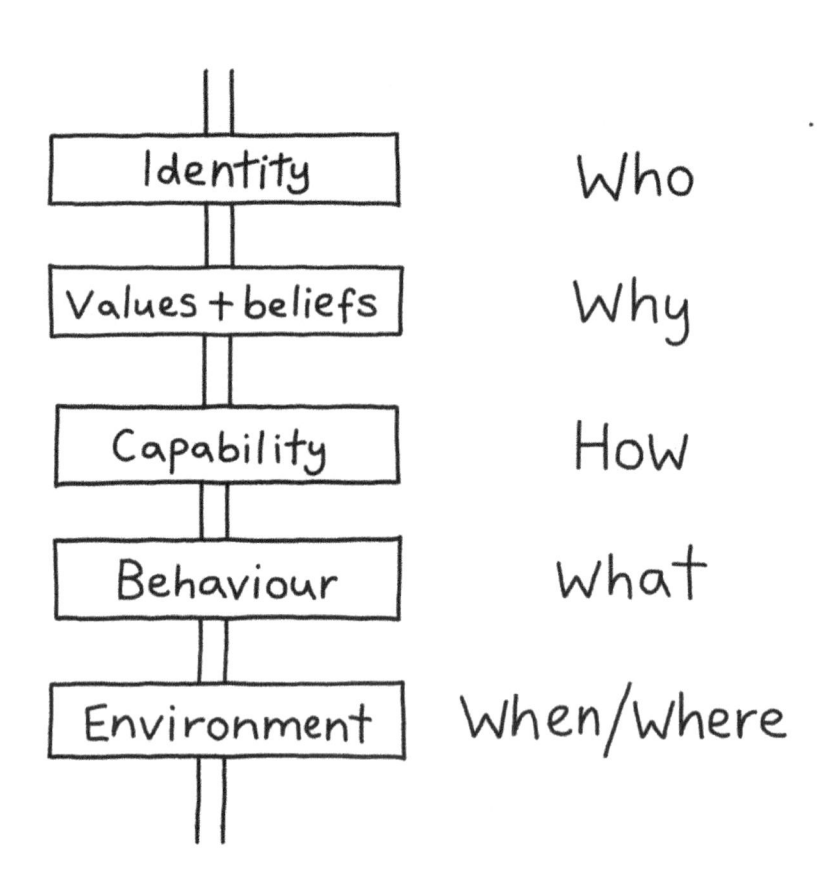

Identity	Who
Values + beliefs	Why
Capability	How
Behaviour	What
Environment	When/Where

Personal alignment

Another area that we can explore when looking at personal effectiveness is alignment. Ghandi once said, 'Happiness is when what you think, what you say, and what you do are in harmony.' We are at our most effective when we have alignment between what we are doing and what we believe to be right.

Alignment can be explored by looking at a phrase, which talks of misalignment, 'I can't do that here'. If we put the emphasis on each of the five different words it reveals five key areas that we need to have aligned in our lives if we are to be truly effective; the environment (the when and the where), behaviour (the what), capability (the how), values and beliefs (the why) and identity (the who).

'I can't do that here' – The environment we are in (When and Where)
When the emphasis is placed on 'here' our issue of alignment is with the place we are in. We have a clear sense about what we can and can't do in different environments e.g. fans at an end of season football match will freely express their emotions but the same people would never be that open at work.

It has been estimated that up to 50% of our behaviour is influenced by the environment we are in. We create unwritten rules for what's acceptable at different times or in different places. These rules form subconsciously as people interact in a certain place and then become group norms as to 'what goes around here'. Although unwritten, you soon get to know if you have stepped outside of a social norm. Try sitting near to someone in an empty railway carriage if you want to test this out. You will get some very clear feedback, either indirectly or directly! If we are to be effective, we need to have a good sense of the unwritten rules for a particular place and feel comfortable operating within these.

'I can't do that here' – The behaviour (What)
When the emphasis is placed on 'that' our issue of alignment is with what we are being asked to do. The most common cause of misalignment at the behaviour level is that we are unclear about exactly what we are supposed to be doing. This lack of clarity can be brought about by failing to check how we have understood a message. You need to get in the habit of checking understanding of key messages by summarizing what has been said. It is not, 'Have you understood?' but 'What have you understood?'

Developing Excellence

1) Match the person with the right capabilities to the right job

2) Develop latent capability to excellence

3) Work around weaknesses

Nobody will be great at everything!

'I can't <u>do</u> that here' – *The capability (How)*
When the emphasis is placed on 'do' our issue of alignment is about a lack of skills or ability. Every person has unique capabilities and weaknesses. Our capabilities are down to the luck of the draw i.e. the body and brain we were born with, and how much we put into developing our potential. If you are asked to do a task that you have no ability to do, you will be fundamentally misaligned. The common-sense principles here are to fit the right person to the right job and to make sure they are properly developed.

Most organisations seem to work to the well-intentioned but misplaced idea of 'wouldn't it be great if our staff were all brilliant at everything'. Hence, usually once a year, everyone goes through the ritual of writing down all the things that they are not good at and resolve to have these improved by the end of the year. Most of the same areas or themes keep reappearing as the individual probably has no latent capability in this area. It can be soul destroying.

Sports teams striving for excellence seem to work to a different philosophy. They seek to match the person, who has the right core capabilities, to the role that they will need to perform in the team. They then seek to develop this latent capability to excellence. If you want to give yourself the best opportunity to perform then do the same. Seek roles that play to your core capabilities and then have a development plan that focuses on developing your strengths to excellence. You will never be brilliant in every area. Working effectively in a team will allow you to offset your weaknesses with others strengths.

Interestingly if you look at your weaknesses you will often see that they come about from an overplayed strength. For example, if you have a strength in analytical thinking you may come across as cold and calculating if this is overplayed. You need to be careful in addressing an area of weakness that you don't lose the strength by overcompensating.

'I <u>can't</u> do that here' – *The belief or our values (Why)*
We are now going much deeper into ourselves. When the emphasis is placed on 'can't' the issue of alignment is about our values and our beliefs. Misalignment at this level is going to have a significant impact on your personal effectiveness. Our values are formed as we grow up and come from a whole range of influences from the world that we live in. We can find it difficult to articulate our values but we clearly know if they have been violated from a strong sense of right and wrong. Imagine for a moment how

The confidence Spiral

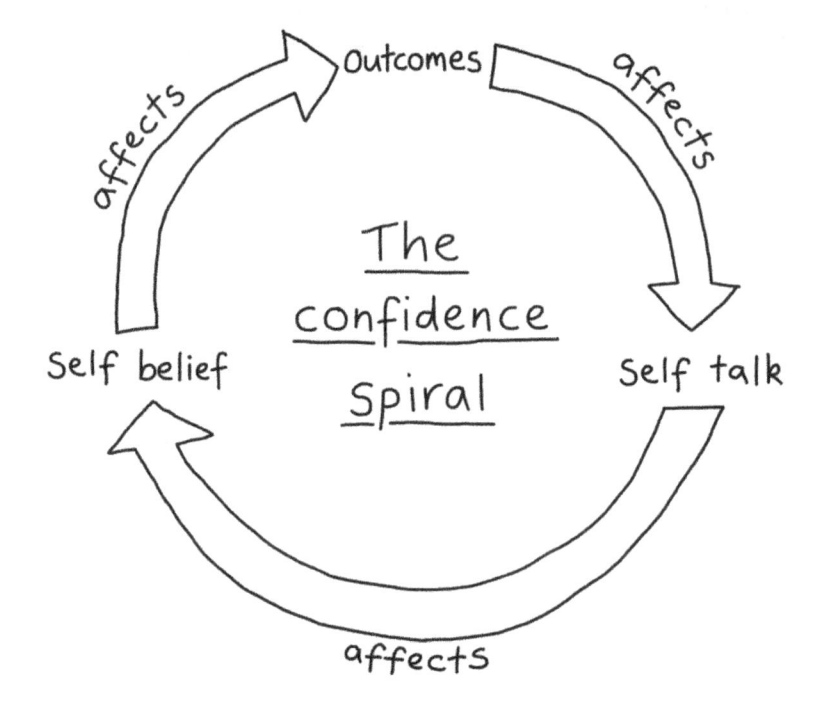

Outcomes *affects* Self talk *affects* Self belief *affects* Outcomes

you would feel if I asked you, or worse still tried to make you, do something that you thought was against your values. Our values rarely change, thus being asked to do something that compromises these, is going to be very uncomfortable and in all likelihood unsustainable!

Our beliefs sit just below our values but also greatly influence our behaviour. It might be said that 'we behave what we believe'. It's not what you say but what you do that reveals your true self. One of the beliefs that most affects our alignment is the belief of whether something is possible or not. The less we believe something is possible, the more misaligned we will be. The self-sorting nature of belief means that we look for things that support our belief. If we believe something is not possible we will notice all the things that are not working. This can lead to a negative downward spiral that only goes to increase our sense of misalignment.

'I can't do that here' – Identity (Who)
When we place the emphasis on 'I' the issue of alignment is to do with our sense of identity or who we are. At the heart of personal effectiveness is a strong foundation of self-confidence and positive self-worth, a sense of 'I am ok'. The more you lose that sense of self-worth, the more misaligned you will feel and the more difficult it will be to perform to your best.

To maintain a positive sense of self, you need to make every effort to divorce outcomes, what you have achieved, from who you are. It is very easy if things are not going well to make the connection, 'my results are rubbish therefore I am rubbish.' This can quickly lead to a downward spiral of worsening performance and declining self-confidence (see over). It may seem subtle but there is a huge difference in your self-talk between 'what I am doing is not good enough' and 'I am not good enough'.

Working with alignment
There are two critical areas to consider in managing yourself; self-awareness and self-management. We need to know where we are in terms of alignment, (self-awareness), and then be able to do something about it, (self-management).

Self-awareness
A useful analogy for personal alignment is your spine. Anybody who has ever struggled with back problems will know that you need to have all your discs in line if you are to be physically effective. If you have a misaligned

Problems of misalignment

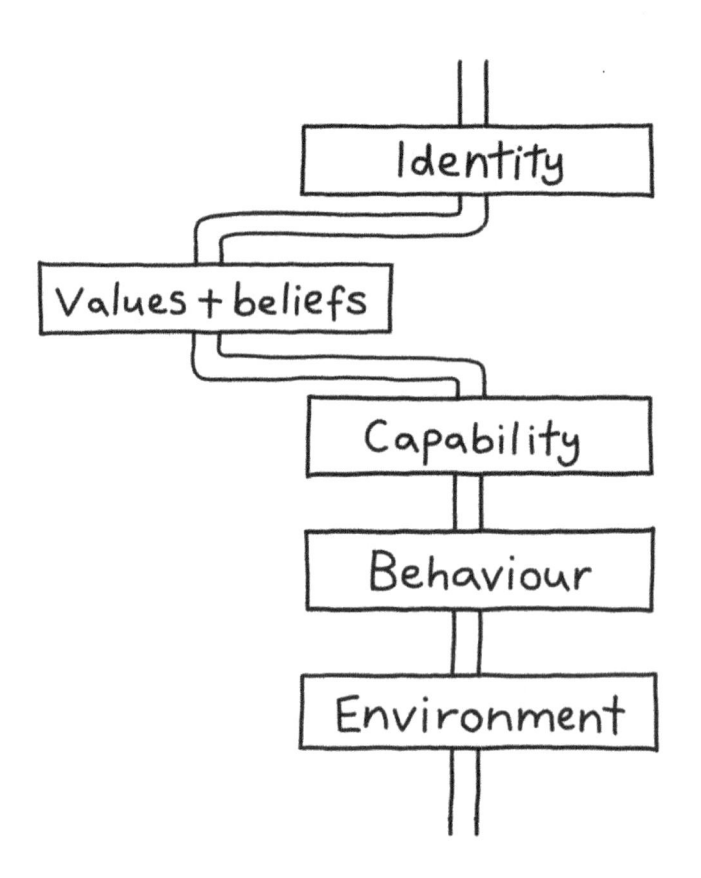

```
        Identity
Values + beliefs
        Capability
        Behaviour
        Environment
```

'Being asked to do something out of line with your values + beliefs'

or defective disc it will cause you problems. It also makes a huge difference where in your spine the problem is. As you go up the spine the problems get worse. The same is true for personal alignment e.g. a problem with the environment you are in will be frustrating but if the problem is leading to misalignment with your values and beliefs, you will be deeply affected.

The analogy of the spine continues further. Your body will tell you that you have a problem with the alignment of your spine through feeling pain. Your brain will tell you that you have a problem with personal alignment through feeling emotions. Think of a time when you were doing something when you were completely aligned i.e. you were in the right place at the right time, you knew exactly what you needed to be doing, you had the capability to do it and it was totally in line with your values, beliefs and a sense of who you are. Now contrast that with a time when you were misaligned i.e. you had been asked to do something that you thought was wrong or that you couldn't do.

What do you notice? Commonly when you have positive alignment you feel almost at peace with yourself, a sense of contentment and purpose. In this state, you are at your most resourceful. If problems occur, you get them sorted. Misalignment on the other hand causes increasing levels of frustration and discontentment. As the frustration grows so your resourcefulness decreases. To maintain performance when you are misaligned takes a huge effort and it becomes tempting just to give up.

It is ironic that we often try to suppress our feelings when in fact they are there to keep us healthy. We seem to have developed the idea, especially at work, that we need to be devoid of emotion if we are to remain effective. In fact, quite the opposite is true! If you are to be truly effective you need to tune in to how you are feeling, know why you are feeling that way and be able to do something about it.

In diagnosing why you are feeling the way that you are, you can use the five levels of alignment to identify where the problem might be by using the questions that accompany each level i.e. Is my problem: -

- The environment – where I am?
- What I have to do?
- How I can do it?
- Why I should do it?
- A sense of fit with who I am?

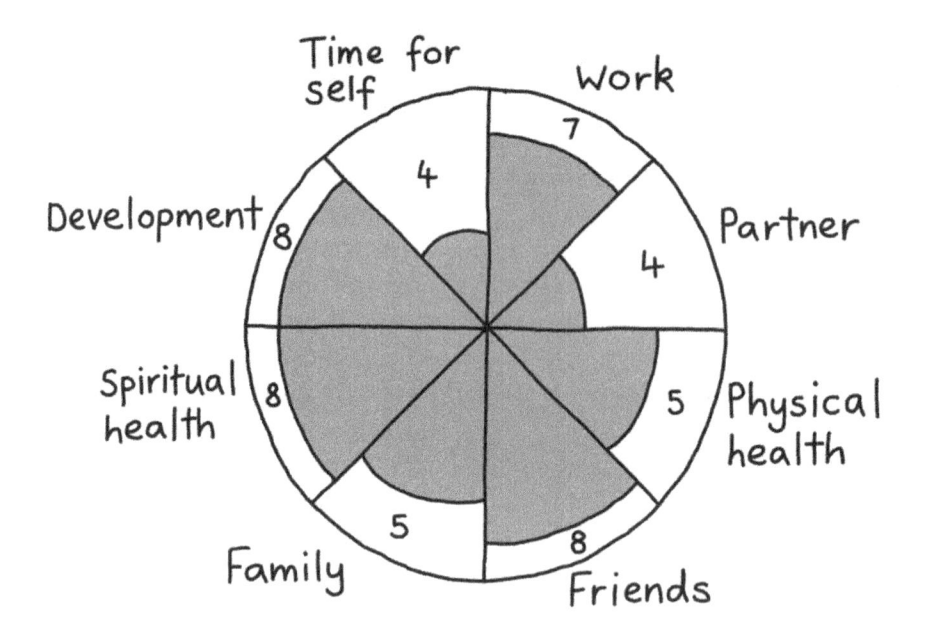

Time for self: 4
Work: 7
Partner: 4
Physical health: 5
Friends: 8
Family: 5
Spiritual health: 8
Development: 8

Life balance wheel

Life Balance Wheel

One further diagnostic tool that I have found useful in understanding why I am feeling the way I am, is the Life Balance Wheel. You will be most effective if you have balance across all the important parts of your life after all, 'All work and no play makes Jack a very unhappy boy!'

To explore your life balance, you divide the 'wheel' up into segments that represent the important parts of your life. You then rate each area out of ten as to how happy you are with this area. You can then join up the segments to give you your 'wheel'. The lumpier the edge is, the worse the wheel will run and so to your life will be less effective. The demands of life mean that it is never possible to pay equal attention to all parts of your life at the same time. Life is like spinning plates; you continually need to move from one aspect of your life to another to ensure that nothing gets dropped. Spending 10 minutes every 2-3 months to reflect on the present state of your life balance can avoid you creating significant problems in your life.

Self-management

We have seen how important personal alignment is to our effectiveness and sense of wellbeing. However, our personal alignment will fluctuate throughout the day as we are confronted by life's challenges. As I mentioned when looking at the Box1/Box 2 balance, the problem is not so much if we lose alignment but how quickly we get it back. The key to personal effectiveness is to be able to do something to regain alignment when you notice that it has been lost. Some useful hints and tips in this are as follows.

Focus on things that you have an influence over

There are many things that may concern you and have an impact on your sense of personal alignment. Some of these things you will be able to influence, some you will not. If you focus on the former it will just make you more frustrated. If you focus on the issues that you can influence you will make progress. Whilst you won't make your life perfect, you will make it better.

A ══causes══▷ B

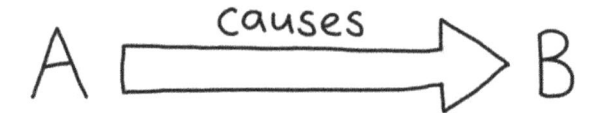

Two dimensional thinking

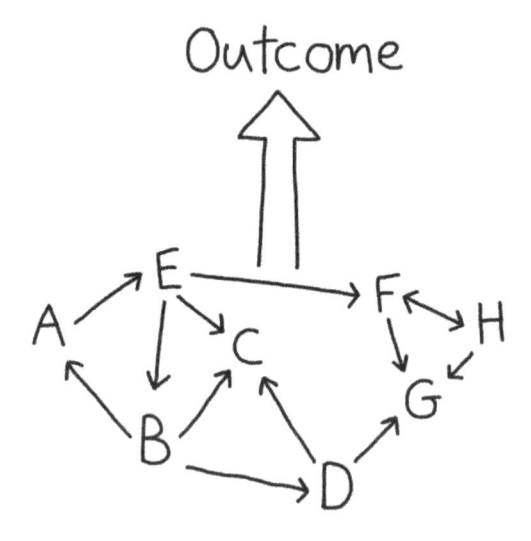

Outcome
⇧

A → E → F ← H
 ↘ ↓ ↙ ↓ ↙
  B → C   G
   ↘ ↗ ↖
     → D →

Three dimensional thinking

(Multiple factors can lead to a certain outcome)

Expand your thinking

We are conditioned to think in a very two-dimensional, simple cause and effect way. If we have a problem we often look for the 'thing' that has caused this. In looking for the cause of the problem we also only look at what has happened in the recent past. Life is more complex than this. The problems we face are caused by multiple reasons, some of which may have come from things that happened a long time ago. The issues with stress that I described at the start of this chapter weren't down to one thing that happened in my life at that time, but were a result of a whole number of factors, some that had been running for several years.

It can also be very easy to look more at what other people have been doing than our own actions. We do this to protect our self-esteem. If we have a problem, it is far more comfortable to point the finger at someone else rather than ourselves. The very fact that you are experiencing a problem must mean that you are part of it in some way.

Know what is important and don't lose sight of it

In many ways prevention is better than the cure. One of the biggest reasons that we lose our personal alignment is because we lose sight of the things that are most important to us. It is a commonly used adage that no one on their death beds ever says that they wished that they had spent more time at work! Sadly, it often takes big things to happen in our lives, like sickness or the death of someone close to us, for us to re-evaluate our lives and recognise that we have lost sight of what is important to us. If you want to remain truly effective, make sure that you take time out regularly to reflect on what is important to you and to check how your life matches up to this.

Personal effectiveness knows no boundaries. Things that are happening at home will affect what is happening at work and vice versa. If we are looking at personal effectiveness we must look at the whole of our lives. The better all the parts of our lives are aligned the more effective we will be in any role, be that a leader, a trainer, a parent, a partner, a friend etc.

Ideas for Action
Box 2 Checklist
Use the checklist below to review your Box 2 activity.

Box 2 Checklist				
Personal development	Y/N	**Personal Reflection**	Y/N	
Defined goals for your development		Weekly reflection on effectiveness		
Specific actions for week/month set		Weekly reflection Box 1-2 balance		
Personal Effectiveness		**Planning**		
Weekly check of lifestyle		Clear 3/6/12 month goals set		
Quarterly review of life balance		Monthly review of plans		
Team Development		**Organisational Capability**		
Team dynamic issues identified		Development needs identified		
½ year team development session		Monthly development activities set		
Process Review		**Key Change Initiative**		
Process issues identified		Key change initiative identified		
Monthly root cause analysis session		Weekly steps for change set		
Stakeholder Review		**Organisational Clarity**		
Quarterly stakeholder feedback		Purpose & Goals understood by all		
Monthly - develop key relationships		Quarterly – organisation alignment?		
Strategic review		**Prevention**		
Clear strategic goals identified		Quarterly – identify potential risks		
Quarterly strategic review		Quarterly – contingency planning?		

Personal Challenges
1. Improve your self-awareness by tracking how you are feeling at 3 different points per day for one week.
2. Improve your life balance by defining and reviewing what success looks like in the different roles that you have in your life. Identify actions to maintain a healthy life balance.

Summary of personal effectiveness
- To be an effective leader you must first be able to manage yourself
- The key elements in managing yourself are self-awareness (knowing where you are in terms of alignment) and self-management (being able to change things to improve your alignment)
- Your future success will be built on Box 2, proactive activities.
- The problems you are experiencing today come from the Box 2 activity you failed to do yesterday
- Achieving a Box 2 balance requires discipline and determination
- Hints of how to break free from the 'Box trap' include: -
  o Be clear about what's important
  o Create specific goals for Box 2 activities
  o Build your diary around Box 2 activities
  o Turn Box 2 activities into specific actions
  o Commit to Box 2 activities
  o Don't mix Box 1 and Box 2 activities and time
  o Schedule regular time to reflect on your Box1/Box 2 balance
- The five key areas that we need have aligned are: -
  o Identity - fitting the sense of who we are
  o Values & Beliefs - alignment with what we believe is right
  o Capability - alignment with what we can do
  o Behaviours - clarity about what we should be doing
  o Environment - fitting the place and the time
- We all have unique strengths and weaknesses. Develop your strengths to excellence and work around your weaknesses.
- Personal effectiveness is built on a sense of 'I am ok.'
- We know where we are in terms of alignment through our feelings.
- Listen to a 'niggle', we are very good at ignoring issues of misalignment. Sort it out before it sorts you out. Long term misalignment can seriously damage your health.
- We need to look at all areas of our life if we are to have positive alignment and balance. Issues in one part of your life will affect other areas.

Chapter 11
Effective Influence

You won't be effective in your influence unless you are open to influence yourself

It seemed that Dave's manager was immune to The Force!

Here's the thing. You cannot fail to have an influence on other people. You might not have the influence that you want to have, but if you are in the same room as another person, you will be influencing them.

Picture this scene. Highlights of a certain sporting event are playing on the telly, highlights that I have been looking forward to all day. My wife sees this as the ideal time to have a chat, after all as I am told, 'The commentary is not important if you can see the pictures!' I am somewhat torn, I want to watch the telly but I know the likely response if I push it! Probably something along the lines of, 'I see, so some stupid rugby match is more important than me, is it?!' Even though I have been delivering soft skills training for over 15 years and should know better, I try to blag it. With one eye on the telly, no let's be honest with both eyes on the telly, I mutter the immortal husband's line, 'No, I am listening, go on.'

225

An Outbreak of Common Sense

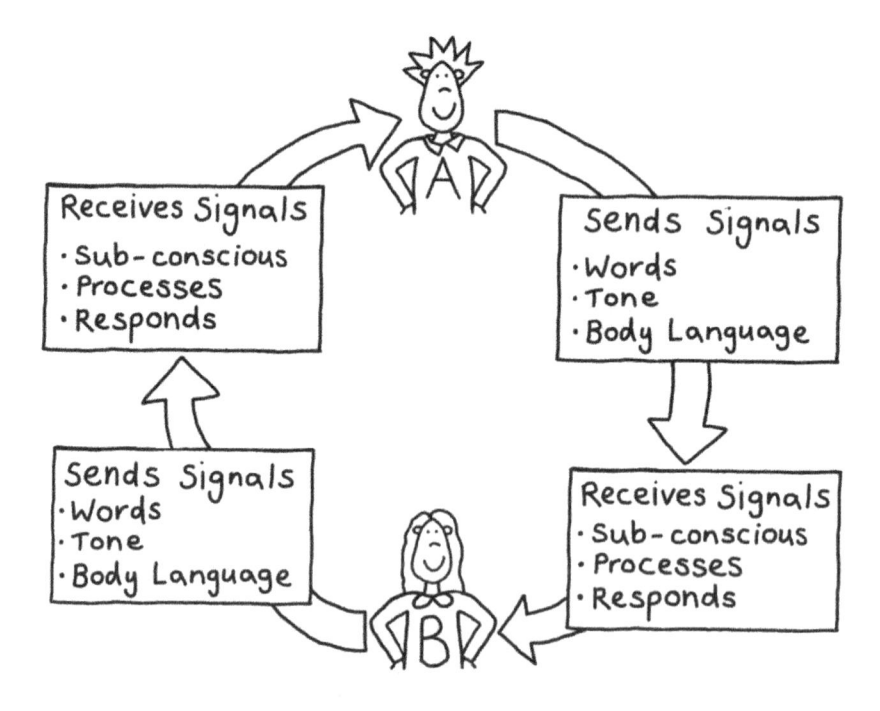

Sends Signals
- Words
- Tone
- Body Language

Receives Signals
- Sub-conscious
- Processes
- Responds

Sends Signals
- Words
- Tone
- Body Language

Receives Signals
- Sub-conscious
- Processes
- Responds

You don't need a degree in psychology to know what happens next! Even though my words are saying I am listening, my tone and my body language are quite clearly saying something else. Something more like, 'I really don't want to talk right now. I want to watch the rugby!!!'

Sound familiar? It is an easy trap to fall into. How many times have you tried to have a conversation with someone whilst they are still looking at their computer screen. 'Go ahead, I'm listening,' they mutter whilst merrily continuing to click away. Rubbish! They might be hearing what you are saying but the message that they are putting out is, 'What's on my screen is more important than you right now.'

The nature of influence

All the time we are sending out signals to other people. We do this in several ways which can be grouped in three main areas; our body language, our tone of voice and the actual words that we might use. You can see from the story above that the biggest impact comes from body language, next comes tone of voice, with words having the least immediate impact.

Even without thinking about it, we live in a continual cycle of sending, receiving, interpreting and responding to signals (see over). Say person A walks into a room, meets person B and says something to them. Person A sends signals in all three areas, words, tone and body language. Because there are millions of signals hitting our senses in any moment, person B filters out certain signals subconsciously. By its very nature this filtering process is subjective. A quick illustration of this; have you ever bought a car only to notice the next day there now seems to be hundreds of the very same model on the road? Has there been a sudden surge in the numbers of this vehicle on the road? No. It's just your subconscious is now filtering for them because it is like your new car.

Once person B has filtered the information, they add meaning and from this react and send signals back to person A. If they like what they have noticed they respond positively, if not, they will be more guarded and negative in their reaction. All this happens in fractions of a second with barely a moment of conscious thought. When you consider the subjective nature of influence it is a surprise that we manage to interact as well as we do, the opportunities for misunderstanding are huge.

Have you ever been in a situation when you have tried to communicate one thing but this has been completely misunderstood by the other person? It feels like the message was fine when it left you but by the time

The Heart of Influence

1) **Authenticity**
   You need to be true to who you are and what you believe

2) **Mutual respect**
   I'm ok and you're ok

3) **Mutual rights**
   We both have the right to seek to get what we want/need

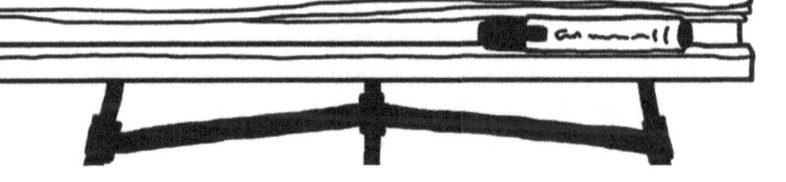

it got to the other person it had changed completely! The difference between our impact and our intent can be a huge source of personal frustration. So, let's look at some practical things that we can do to try to have the influence we want.

The heart of effective influence

When we are proactively seeking to influence another person, we are seeking to bring about a change in how they think and/or what they are doing. At the heart of effective influence are three core principles; authenticity, mutual respect and mutual rights.

Authenticity

Effective influence can't be done by using clever tricks or pre-prepared techniques, despite the efforts of most fast food chains and call centres to try to prove otherwise! Imagine welcoming someone to your home. Would you need a script or some handy prompts to remind you to smile? So why would we expect some processed word pattern or approach to come across as genuine in a work context?

I regularly use a pet shop in town. The staff are friendly and knowledgeable and talk freely as they deal with any query I might have about pet care. However as soon as I get to the till they suddenly turn into strange customer service robot and switch into 'script' mode. 'Did you find everything that you were looking for today?' they always ask on the first sweep of the bar code reader. You can tell that they have been told to say this and that they have probably said it a hundred times before that day. It comes across as inauthentic and it leaves me feeling processed.

Any perceived mismatch in body language, tone or words will come across as inauthentic. No matter how much you might try to mask it, your true feelings and beliefs will come out in your communication. As a leader seeking a positive influence, authenticity is everything. If you try to communicate something that you don't really believe in it can be very damaging. People will hear you saying one thing but communicating something else. When people perceive incongruence in the message, trust alarm bells start to ring and they will become cautious, guarded and withdraw from the relationship. If you want to have an effective influence people must trust you and your message.

'But,' I hear you cry, 'this is all well and good for you in theoryland. In the real world, you don't always get the luxury of believing in every

An Outbreak of Common Sense

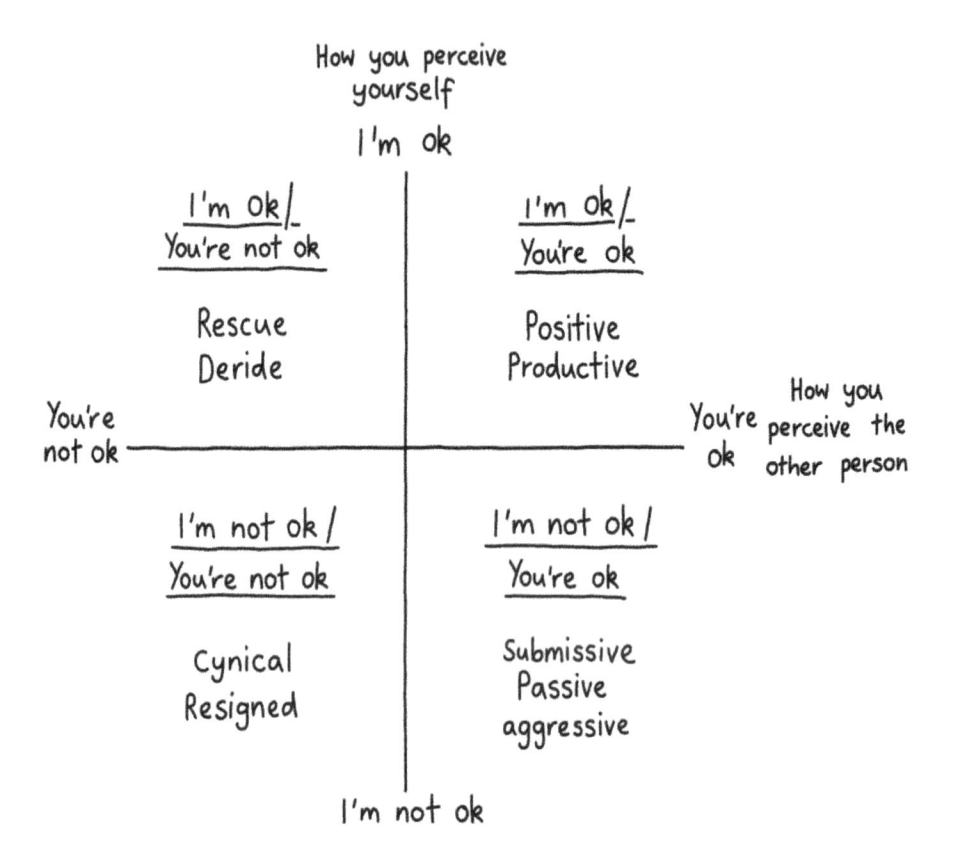

```
                    How you perceive
                        yourself
                         I'm ok
                           |
        I'm Ok/             |        I'm Ok/
        You're not ok       |        You're ok
                           |
         Rescue             |        Positive
         Deride             |        Productive
                           |                        How you
You're                     |                You're  perceive the
not ok ────────────────────┼──────────────── ok     other person
                           |
        I'm not ok/         |        I'm not ok/
        You're not ok       |        You're ok
                           |
         Cynical            |        Submissive
         Resigned           |        Passive
                           |        aggressive
                           |
                      I'm not ok
```

directive you have to implement!' I get this but if you seek to communicate things that you don't believe in, you will undermine your position as a leader. To remain authentic and personally effective in your relationships with your people you have three choices; 1) You could push back with your leaders to challenge whether this really is the right thing to do. 2) You could seek further rationale as to why this is the right thing to do, so that you can truly believe in the message. 3) You could speak honestly about your reservations but seek to align to a different value or driver e.g. 'I won't lie to you; I am not sure if this is the right thing to do but we must be professional and give it our very best shot.'

Mutual respect
The idea of mutual respect can best be explored through the idea of 'I am OK, you are OK' (see over). This idea was first put forward by Eric Berne and further developed by Thomas Harris and Franklin Ernst. Effective influence can only happen if you feel ok in yourself and you also believe that the other person is ok. Any other position will lead to negative or unhelpful behaviours.

If you are feeling ok about yourself but you think that the other person is not, it will lead you to either try to rescue them or to deride them. If you are not feeling ok about yourself but think the other person is ok, it will lead you to being passive and doing everything they want, or for you to become passive/aggressive. This might best be summed up in the phrase, 'It's alright for you!' If I am not feeling ok about myself and the other person, it is likely that I will become cynical and resigned; 'There's no hope for either of us!'

Mutual rights
The third core principle for effective influence is mutual rights; both parties have the right to seek to try to meet their needs/wants. One of the biggest obstacles I come across when I am working with people looking to enhance the effectiveness of their influence, is they don't feel comfortable in asking for what they want. We are often scripted from an early age with sayings such as, 'I wants don't get!' It is ok to seek to get what you want as long as this comes with the recognition that the other person has this right as well. If your influence stance is only ever about you getting what you want, you will soon come to a standoff where no one is prepared to change. You will only be effective in your influence if you are open to influence yourself.

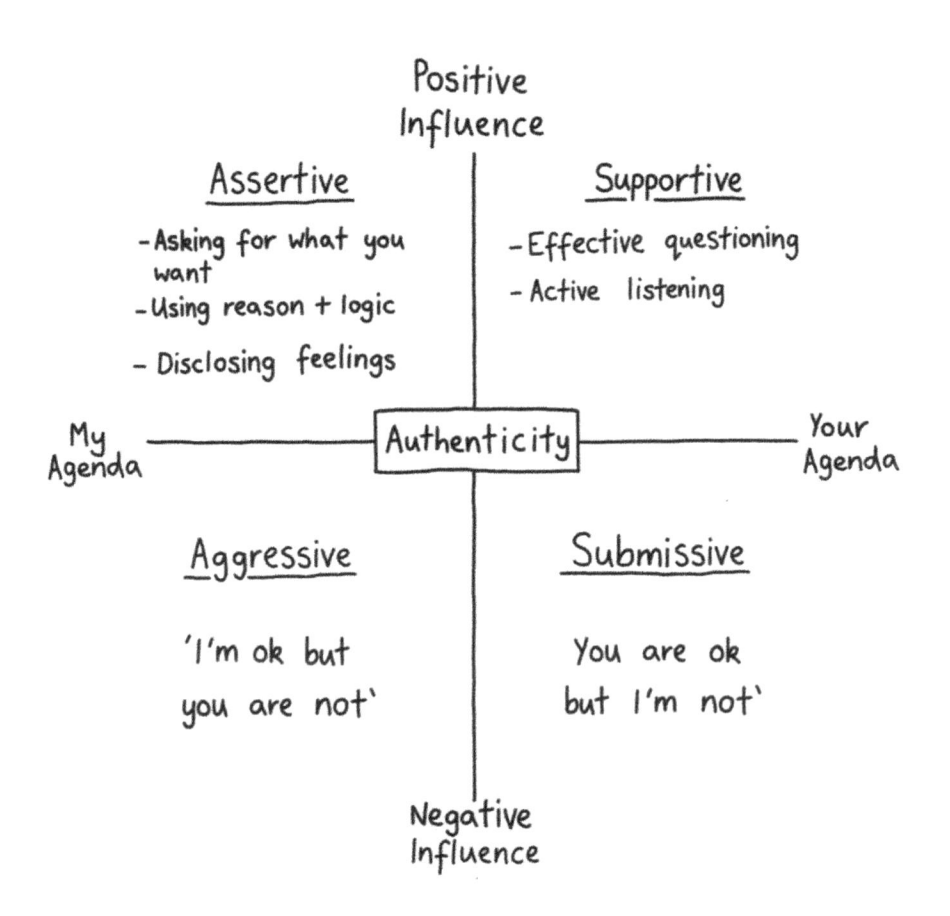

Positive Influence

Assertive
- Asking for what you want
- Using reason + logic
- Disclosing feelings

Supportive
- Effective questioning
- Active listening

My Agenda ——————— | Authenticity | ——————— Your Agenda

Aggressive
'I'm ok but you are not'

Submissive
You are ok but I'm not'

Negative Influence

Effective influence behaviours

We can use these three core principles to create a framework in which to operate to have an effective influence. At the centre of the framework is authenticity. To have an effective influence you must be honest and be true to who you are and what you believe. Building on this you can have either a positive or a negative influence based on the principle of mutual respect. Positive influence, above the line, happens when both parties feel ok about the interaction. Negative influence, below the line, happens when one party is not ok about the interaction. If I am ok with something but you are not, then I will have been aggressive in pursuing my agenda. If you are ok but I am not, then I will have been submissive i.e. I will have done what you wanted but not felt happy with it.

If we are to pursue an agenda of mutual rights to both seek to get what we want, our approach to influence will need to be a balance of assertive behaviours, pursuing what I want, and supportive behaviours, seeking to understand and accommodate what the other party wants.

Supportive influence

Supportive influence is working to understand and accommodate someone else's agenda. You might question how doing this will help you getting what you want. A strong principle in relationships is reciprocity. For a relationship to work there needs to be a balance of give and take. The act of genuinely seeking to understand and accommodate someone else's agenda builds credit. People are much more likely to be open to influence from us if we have demonstrated a genuine desire to work with them. We can explore supportive influence through two core behaviours; effective questioning and active listening.

Effective questioning

If you are going to really understand someone else's position you should get off your own agenda. Frequently when people are in an influence situation their questions will be framed by their agenda i.e. they will explore areas that are of interest to them. An analogy that I like to use to illustrate effective questioning is to think of a tree (see next page). You start with the trunk by seeking to understand the broad area of interest that the other person wants to talk about and then pursue the detail of this by exploring the various branches that define this area. For example, one of your team might want to explore future career options. This might break down into

An Outbreak of Common Sense

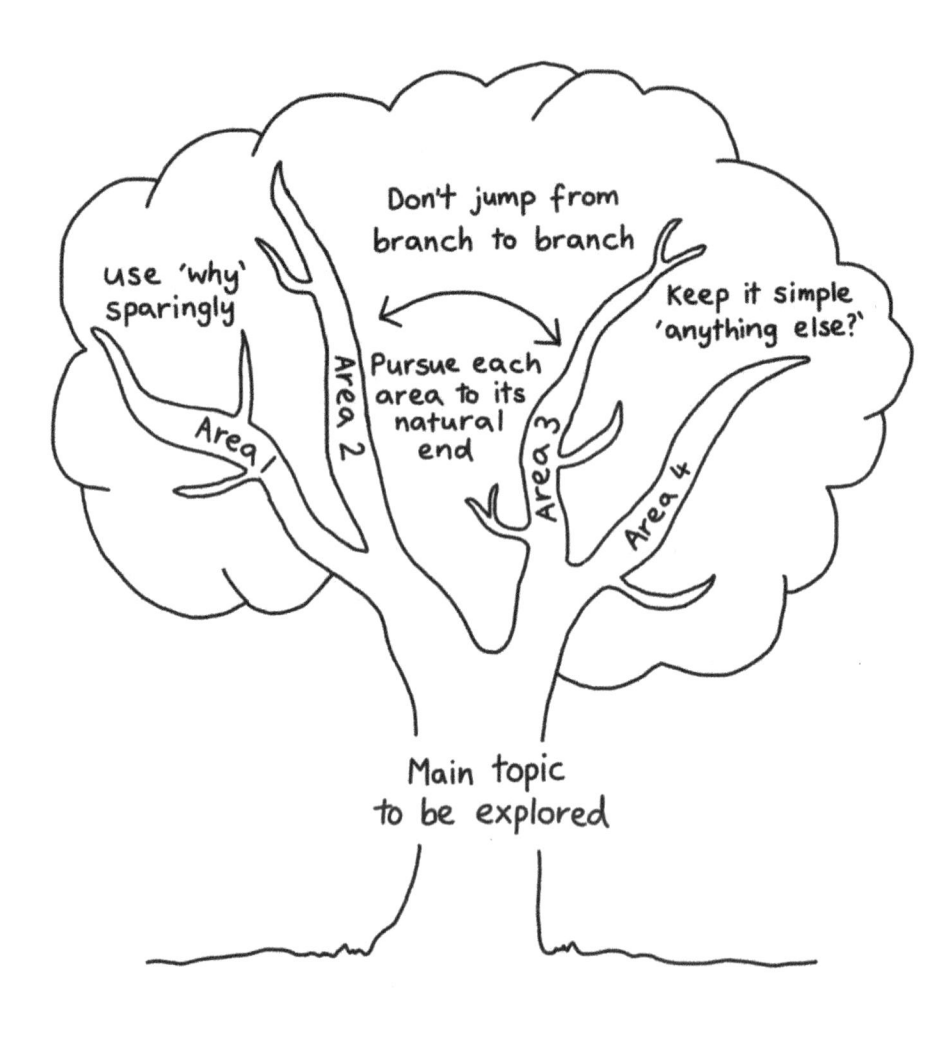

- use 'why' sparingly
- Don't jump from branch to branch
- Keep it simple 'anything else?'
- Pursue each area to its natural end
- Area 1
- Area 2
- Area 3
- Area 4

Main topic to be explored

Effective Questioning

opportunities within their current role, possible training and development options, understanding career options and understanding what makes them tick.

When exploring the other person's agenda, you should avoid jumping from one area (branch) to another. You should stay with a subject as long as the other person wants to explore it before moving on. You should also be careful not to be seen to be challenging their right to a certain opinion. The question 'why' can easily lead to this. 'Why do you think something?' can easily be interpreted by the other person as, 'Why on earth do you think that?!' It is best to be sparing in the use of 'why' maybe using options like, 'What's behind your thinking on that?' or 'How have you come to that view?'

One last tip I would offer on effective questioning is keep it simple. I often see people so busily trying to think up the next question that they completely stop listening to the other person. Using prompts like, 'anything else' or 'what else' can be very helpful in keeping deeper exploration simple.

Active Listening

Let's get something straight from the start; active listening is not about nodding your head and making encouraging 'I'm listening' type noises! Another statement of common sense is that if we are to understand other people we must really listen to them. This is easily said but rarely done well. We shouldn't confuse politely letting someone finish their point with listening. Often people in meetings are in one of two states, either speaking or waiting to speak! In most interactions, there isn't a whole load of listening going on.

To really listen to someone takes considerable effort. You need to exercise self-control in not jumping in with your own point. You also need to give them your full attention and tune in not only to what they are saying but also in how they are saying it. Listening is done with with both our eyes and our ears. You need to both listen to the words and tone and notice the signals coming from their body language. To really listen well you therefore must give the other person your full attention and avoid distractions

It is somewhat ironic that in the name of connecting people better, technological changes have led to a massive increase in communication that discourages people from being in the same room as each other. A friend of mine phoned me up once absolutely spitting nails about an email she had just received. It simply said, 'You weren't at your desk at 6:00 so I have sent

An Outbreak of Common Sense

Effective Listening

1) Give the other person your full attention

2) Use regular summaries 'So what you're saying is...'

3) Reflect feeling 'You seem frustrated about this'

you this.' You could read that message in any number of ways from just a factual statement to one with a highly judgemental tone about her commitment. She took it to mean the latter and was extremely unhappy.

I am often asked to help people work in 'virtual' teams i.e. groups of people who need to behave as a team but work in different locations. My reply to this is that people can only develop their relationships so far if they never meet. If you met someone on a dating website, you would probably need to meet them if you wanted to take the relationship further! Whilst technologies like video conferencing do allow you to see other people's body language the camera greatly stilts people's natural behaviour. On a Skype call I spend most of my time wondering who the old fart in the corner of my screen is! The three top tips I would offer in listening are: -

1. Give the person your full attention
   Put down anything that may distract you and suspend your desire to make your own point.
2. Use regular summaries
   'So, what you are saying is ....' Not only does this help you to clarify your understanding but also shows them you have been listening.
3. Reflect their feeling
   Pick up the subtext of what they are communicating in how they are communicating it i.e. body language and tone. 'You seem (emotion e.g. fed up, enthusiastic, angry) about that.' Keep your reflections short and punchy and let the other person say the next thing. They will either confirm that is how they are feeling and probably speak more about it, or correct you if you have got it wrong but then say how they are really feeling.

Assertive behaviours

The judgement of whether you are being assertive or not is made by the people you are interacting with and comes from how they perceive your behaviour. If you draw up a scale of assertiveness from 1-10, with passive at one end and aggressive at the other end, you will find every person will have a preferred place in which they operate. And here's the problem. The other person judges if you are being assertive relative to their own position. You, just being yourself, could come across as passive to one person and aggressive to another without changing anything that you are doing! Being assertive can't be defined by a narrow group of behaviours.

Little things make a big difference

I once worked with a senior manager who was extremely frustrated about a particular member of staff. Nothing that she did seemed to get through to him. I explored the situation a bit further and asked her to play out a normal meeting with this member of staff. She had very high levels of energy, talked fast and sat very upright and towards the front of her chair. The member of staff was much more laid back and almost slouched in his chair; this she found very frustrating. As she tried harder to get her point across, her energy levels would increase and she would talk faster and louder. In response to this the member of staff would become increasingly laid back.

This was a classic mismatch of someone who normally operated at about seven on the assertive behaviours scale with someone else that operated closer to a three. As her frustration grew the gap grew wider; as she went up the scale, he went down. My advice to her was to 'slouch' a bit i.e. sit back further in her chair. Not only would this tone down her body language but also would slow down the speed of her delivery. It is quite difficult to be excitable sitting back in your chair. Her immediate response was, 'I don't do slouching!'

'I know,' I said, 'but neither does he do Tigger on speed!' We persevered and tried a few mock runs of working with this member of staff with her working from a slightly less energised position. She left the programme still not fully convinced but committed to at least trying it out.

A few weeks later I received a really positive phone call. 'It worked!' she told me excitedly. She had tried the different approach and their relationship had been transformed. As she had toned down her initial impact he had responded positively and become increasingly engaged with her. What had originally been a vicious cycle of frustration had turned into a virtuous cycle of the two people responding positively to each other. This might seem strange to you but when it comes down to effective influence little things can make a huge difference.

Effective Influence

If you want to be seen as assertive you will need to change your approach with different people. A good analogy for this is going for a walk with somebody. Even though people will have different stride lengths and preferred speeds for walking they naturally fall into step with each other. When we are in rapport with someone else we 'fall into step' with them matching their body language and tone. This means that you need to change how you are behaving to do this. Staying the same will not get the results you want; for one person, it may be too much, for another it may be too little.

Being flexible in your approach might not be easy for you as it may push you out of your comfort zone. In any influence situation, however, the only behaviour you can guarantee to change is your own. If one party doesn't change, we will never 'fall into step' and build rapport. An example of this is detailed in the story over page, 'Little things can make a big difference.'

When I am entering a situation where I feel that I need to be assertive I make a conscious effort to remember three C's; be clear, calm and concise. These provide a good foundation for using one of the three assertive behaviours; Asking for what you want, Using reason and logic and Disclosing Feelings.

Asking for what you want

The simplest way to get what you want is to ask for it. As we have already seen, for some people being this direct can be a challenge. Often people over complicate their requests or express them too passively. This leaves the other party unclear about what exactly is being requested and how important it is to the person requesting it. If you come up against resistance it can help to simply repeat the request again. I once had to repeat the same request three times to get a refund on some faulty shoes. I knew I was within my rights so when the shop assistant initially refused I simply restated my request. The calm reassertion of my position made it clear that I was not going to take no for an answer.

Using reason and logic

You may have gathered that I am somewhat suspicious of people using set frameworks and approaches in influence situations. However, just to show that an exception proves every rule, I have found the following framework invaluable in sharpening up my influence skills. This 3-step

Disclosing feelings using Reason and Logic

1) Flag your intention
   'I need to let you know where I am on this'

2) State your feeling with # of reasons
   'I am feeling really frustrated about this for 2 reasons'

3) State your reasons
   'Firstly _ _ _ _ _ _._ _ _ _ _'
   'Secondly _ _ _ _ _._ _ _ _ _'

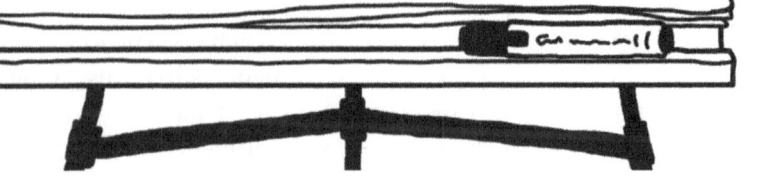

framework maximises your impact by making points in a succinct and logical way.
1. Let people know that you want to make a point e.g. I want to make a point
2. State your point and tell them the number of reasons that support this e.g. I believe that (make your point) for two reasons.
3. Give your reasons numbering them off as you go e.g. These are; 1) .... and 2)...............

If I was using this framework to seek to influence you to use it I might say the following, 'I want to make a point. I believe that you should look to try out this framework for three reasons. Firstly, people will hear your point more clearly as they know what they should be listening for. Second, it will help you in your own thought processes to be clear about what you want to say and why. Third, it will stop you waffling and losing impact.'

Some hints and tips when you are using this approach: -

- Never have more than three reasons. If you haven't convinced them after three reasons you are unlikely to by giving them more. Also, you will probably forget what they are anyway!
- Use body language, such as numbering off your reasons on your fingers, to emphasise your points.
- When you have finished making your point, stop talking. Let it land with the other person and give them space to come back to you with their response.

People often say that this approach feels a bit 'clunky' at first. However, as they become more practiced, invariably they find that it makes a huge difference in their influence. For quieter, more introverted people it encourages them to speak up, for more talkative folk, like myself, it encourages them to be more succinct and impactful. You know when you have cracked it when you find yourself saying to your partner something like, 'I want you to do the washing-up tonight for two reasons. These are………...' Mind you, I must admit that it's at this point my wife usually says, 'Don't try that trainer crap on me!' Some people are just resistant to the power of the Force!

Disclosing feelings

It is rarely helpful to be highly emotional in an influence situation. High emotions will trigger a 'fight or flight' response in the other party, neither of which will lead to a positive outcome. It is however helpful, on

Sources of Power

Power to force change

'I'll do what you want because I have to'

eg. Position
    Knowledge
    Resource
    Reward / Punish

Breeds compliance

Relationship Power

'I'll do what you want because I want to do it for you'

Results from continually treating others with care honesty + respect

Breeds engagement

occasions, to let people know how you are feeling as this will give them a much clearer sense of your position.

To do this effectively you need to be able to communicate your feelings in an unemotional way. Using the reason and logic framework can be a helpful way to do this e.g. 'I want to let you know where I am on this. Right now, I am extremely frustrated at the number of errors we are seeing with this process. This is for two reasons; 1) It's leading to several customer complaints 2) I thought that we had put things in place to solve this problem. What I therefore want is.........................'

Hopefully this has given you a few useful hints and tips about what you can do to have a more effective influence. As with any performance improvement you will only get better if you are prepared to give something a go and stay with it until it feels natural.

Use the power at your disposal wisely

Within any relationship, we will have a certain amount of power at our disposal. Use of this power can bring about change in one of two ways; the person is made to change or the person chooses to change. Examples of the power to force change include being in a position of authority, having control over the allocation of resources, having knowledge or expertise or having the power to reward or punish the other party.

Having the power to force change needs to be used sparingly. People don't like being made to do something. Whilst they might do what you want, the best you can hope for is compliance. When people feel made to do something they tend only to do the bare minimum that they are asked to do. In more extreme cases they may even conspire to fail. Over time if people continually feel made to do things levels of engagement and initiative will fall and the performance of the organisation will suffer.

The power of a positive relationship is a completely different type of power. With relationship power people, will do what you want because they want to do it for you. Building this power comes from consistently demonstrating care, honesty, fairness and respect to the other person. Relationship power leads to engagement. People will go the extra mile because they are doing it for you.

Ideas for action
Reflect on a difficult conversation
Think of a conversation that you had recently that did not go as well as you might have hoped. Take a sheet of paper and divide it into two columns by drawing a vertical line down the middle. In the right-hand column, right out a part of the conversation, as you remember it, as if it were a drama script i.e. I said ...., they said...................

In the left-hand column, right down what you were thinking at different stages of the conversation. As you look at what you have written down reflect on the following questions: -

- How did your thinking affect your responses in the meeting?
- How did your responses affect how the other person behaved?
- What was the basis for your thinking?
- What could you have done differently to produce a more favourable response?
- What steps will you take to improve the situation in the future?

Remember, in any relationship the only person's behaviour you can guarantee to change is your own. If you act differently the relationship will be changed. You need to continue to try different approaches to get the outcome that you want.

Personal challenges
Practise, practise, practise. The greater the range of behaviours and approaches you have at your disposal, the more effective you will be in your influence. The only way that you will feel comfortable with a new approach is to practise it, so next week: -
1. In conversations reflect the feeling you are noticing at least 5x
2. Use reason and logic at least 5x
3. Give 5 pieces of authentic, positive feedback
4. Use 'I want' or disclosing feelings at least 5x
5. Do at least one thing for each person you work with that will improve your relationship with them
6. Make a note as you go long of what you tried and how it worked

Summary of effective influence

- We are always influencing others through the signals we are sending out through our body language, tone and words.
- The three core principles at the heart of effective influence are: -
  - Authenticity – be true to your core values and beliefs
  - Mutual respect – 'I'm OK and You're OK'
  - Mutual rights – We both have the right to seek to get what we want
- If we are to really understand people we have to listen to them. Listening is done as much with our eyes as with our ears.
  - Give the other person your full attention
  - Summarise your understanding of what they have said regularly
  - Reflect the feeling that you are picking up through the tone and body language
- When you are seeking to be assertive remember the three C's
  - Be calm
  - Be clear
  - Be concise
- It is the other person who decides if you are being assertive. You need to flex your approach with different people to have the desired impact
- Use 'reason and logic' when making your point
  - I want to make a point
  - My point is …………… for (1, 2 or 3) reasons
  - These reasons are; 1) ……….. 2) ………... 3) ……………
- Don't try to use 'tricks' or play games when seeking to influence people. Do the basics; demonstrate respect, listen and put your own point over clearly

Melbec Development Ltd

Facilitating transformational change

Effectively engaging people with change is one of the greatest challenges facing leaders in organisations today. Your organisation must keep pace with changes in the world in which you operate. We work with leaders and their organisations to facilitate the change on which the future success of the organisation will be built.

Melbec Development was established in 2006 and is led by Senior Consultant, Robert Funning. We work with a network of associates offering extensive experience in facilitating change and developing leaders, drawn from work internationally with a wide range private and public sector organisations.

Purpose and Motivation

Our professional purpose is to enable individuals and organisations to be more effective and successful by helping them to adapt and align to change in the world around them. Our core drivers are: –

- To make a positive difference for individuals and organisations
- To support individuals and organisations through key points of change
- To create and mutually share success between ourselves, our clients, our partners and suppliers
- To continually learn and encourage others to do likewise through the free exchange of knowledge and perspectives

We work in partnership with our clients, investing time to understand your business, what defines success for you and the challenges that you face. We deliver pragmatic solutions that meet your organisation's needs in a way that your people will relate to.

To find out more please visit our website: -

www.melbecdevelopment.co.uk